BATHROOM BOOK
of
CANADIAN HISTORY

Barbara Smith

BLUE
BIKE
BOOKS

The Publisher: Blue Bike Books

Library and Archives Canada Cataloguing in Publication

Smith, Barbara, 1947–
       The bathroom book of Canadian history / Barbara Smith.

 (Bathroom books of Canada ; 2)
ISBN-13: 978-0-9739116-1-9
ISBN-10: 0-9739116-1-1

       1. Canada—History—Miscellanea. I. Title. II. Series.

FC60.S56 2005   971   C2005-905806-4

Project Director: Audrey McClellan
Illustrations: Roger Garcia
Cover Image: Roger Garcia & Valentino

PC: P5

DEDICATION

For Nancy
for fun
for friendship

ACKNOWLEDGEMENTS

Thanks to Blue Bike Books for the opportunity to explore the "other side" of Canadian history. Thank you to editor Audrey McClellan for sharing her considerable skills on this project. Audrey, your efforts and your pleasant manner were so appreciated. Special thanks to my fellow author Angela Murphy. And, as always, thanks to my family and closest friends. Your very existence makes everything worthwhile.

CONTENTS

BE A SPORT

TAKE ME TO YOUR LEADERS

WORLD WARS AND COLD WAR

PLANES, TRAINS, CAMELS...

ODDS 'N ENDS

INTRODUCTION

Researching this book was a bit like getting to be a kid again. What fun it has been to turn over all the big old rocks and boulders of Canadian history and find the "good" stuff—wriggly and squirmy and dirty though it may have been—hiding underneath.

For instance, did you know that in 1867, when Canada became a country, politicians were paid $6.00 a day and that Sir John A. Macdonald was sometimes sober? Or that Viking explorers used to take exotic (and very dangerous!) souvenirs home from Canada?

Well, at least we all know about the Last Spike—or do we?

What about the ancient (and very confusing) riches a group of prospectors found near Cassiar, British Columbia, during the Cariboo Gold Rush?

And why didn't they teach us this stuff in school?

Fortunately, it's never too late to learn so, sit down and have a read—about Canada's "extra-ordinary" history!

1812
AND ALL THAT

*A trivial collection of significant events,
people and symbols in Canadian history*

YOU CAN GET IT AT THE BAY

NOTHING BIGGER OR OLDER. Most Canadians know that "HBC" stands for Hudson's Bay Company (not "Here Before Christ" as some cynics like to think!). The company was started in 1670. At the time, no one even knew where the HBC's boundaries were. It was the biggest private owner of real estate in the world. Even today the Bay is the oldest chain store in the world.

LET'S MAKE A BIG DEAL OUTA THIS. Real estate moguls are apparently not a new breed. In 1670, King Charles II of England gave most of today's Québec, Ontario, Manitoba, Saskatchewan and Alberta to the Hudson's Bay Company.

KISSIN' COUSINS? He called the land that he'd so generously given away Rupert's Land—after his cousin, Prince Rupert. Guess you had to be there. Maybe Rupert was a swell fellow.

BUY LOW; SELL HIGH. The high-powered deals didn't stop there. In 1869, the Canadian government bought Rupert's Land from the HBC for £300,000. That's a pretty tidy profit—and the world's largest land transaction ever.

BRING US YOUR WOMEN!

*Our quick-thinking forefathers realized
right at the start that it's tough to populate a country
when most of the people in that country are men.*

WHERE THE BOYS ARE. By the mid-1600s, King Louis XIV of France had become very interested in populating New France, but that was going to be tough to do because most of the explorers, fur traders, soldiers and settlers who'd come to Canada were men.

HERE'S AN IDEA. The king decided to entice women to go to the New World. But he didn't want them to be just any sort of women. No sir. Louis XIV chose the settlers' potential wives with great care.

AND THE WINNERS ARE. The future brides were called "Filles du roi" or "Daughters of the king." They were rarely less than 12 years of age or older than 25. Many had to supply a letter of reference from their parish priest before they would be chosen for their new adventure in New France.

EVERYONE WEIGHS IN ON THE NEW SUBJECTS. France's minister of finances, Jean-Baptiste Colbert, must have understood genetics as well as finances because he enthusiastically supported the king's ideas. Colbert declared, "It is important to sow good seed."

MEMO FROM THE BOSS. And Jean Talon, the guy with the corner office in New France, added his own riders to the new immigration policy. He declared that the females sent from the homeland shouldn't be "disgraced by nature" nor "repulsive about their external persons." He also, sensibly, added that they should be "healthy and strong for country work or at least have some inclination to work with their hands."

SHIP 'EM OFF TO SUCCESS. The French government paid to have the lucky ladies shipped from France to New France and also supplied them with dowries. King Louis' plan worked so well that today many Québecers can trace their heritage back to a "daughter of the king."

AND FOR THE WILD WEST. Some 200 years later there was just as great a push to get western Canada populated, but Clifford Sifton, minister of the interior at the time, apparently didn't share the former king of France's standards. Sifton thought "a stout wife" of "a stalwart peasant" "with half a dozen children" was what was needed to settle Canada.

DID YOU  KNOW?

WHAT A LOSS THAT WOULD'VE BEEN! John Molson must've wanted desperately to say "My name is John, and I am Canadian." In 1780, when he was 18 years old, John left England to come to Canada. He almost didn't make it. The ship he was on was lost at sea. Fortunately, John, the future beer king, was pulled from the icy waters and certain death. Our thirsts thank his rescuers!

OLD ABE'S FARM

THE PLAINS OF ABRAHAM. The name has an exotic sound, as if it should be a locale in some far-distant land. The name may have a decidedly unCanadian ring to it, but the Battle of the Plains of Abraham was one of Canada's defining moments.

WOLFE ATTACK! During the 1700s, control of "the colonies" was being volleyed back and forth between the English and the French. Just before breakfast on September 13, 1759, General James Wolfe decided it was time to win one for England. He organized his troops to attack a French fort near Québec City. Not just any French fort, mind you. Wolfe carefully chose a poorly secured one.

SHHH. Then, to bolster his chances, he planned the attack as a surprise.

MONTCALM GETS WIND! Louis-Joseph de Montcalm, the French military leader in the area, got wind of Wolfe's plan, however, and rallied as many of his own troops as he was able to. He probably had about the same number as Wolfe was bringing to the meeting, but the English were all trained soldiers. The French men were mostly militia.

THE BATTLE. Inequalities aside, the two groups marched against each other at about 10:00 in the morning. Fifteen minutes later the fighting was over. More than 1000 soldiers lay dead or injured. Wolfe and his British soldiers had defeated the Marquis de Montcalm and his French troops. Neither victory nor defeat made a lasting impression on either leader, though, because within hours they were both dead.

HOW ABOUT BEST TWO OUT OF THREE? The battle's result wasn't lasting either, for England and France continued to squabble.

MONCKTON OR MONCTON? There were *some* permanent results from the morning's carnage. Wolfe's right-hand man, Lieutenant General Robert Monckton, for instance, had a city in New Brunswick named after him—sort of. You probably know the place as "Moncton," not "Monckton." Those pesky clerical errors will happen!

PALM TREES IN CANADA? Both the French and English commissioned paintings to commemorate their leaders' valiant deaths. Unfortunately, those paintings are even less accurate than the spelling of the English lieutenant general's name! The most famous artistic rendition of Montcalm's death shows a palm tree growing nearby. The painting also depicted Wolfe's death, but has the enemy leader dying in a decidedly less heroic pose.

BETTER LATE THAN NEVER. English artist Benjamin West painted his depiction of Wolfe's death much more favourably— 11 years after an event he hadn't attended.

MORE ARTISTIC LICENCE. Wolfe's image, not surprisingly, is central on West's canvass, carefully lit and extraordinarily dramatic. The great general is surrounded by mourning admirers, including a Native in the pose of The Thinker. This, even though General Wolfe was known to have been disdainful of aboriginal people, probably because they had sided with the French, not the English.

STARVING ARTIST? Stylistic licence aside, West's work was evidently a hit. The painting was so well received that the artist soon dashed off several additional "originals" for wealthy English patrons willing to reward him generously for his highly biased rendition.

WHAT'S IN A NAME? But how did that deadly skirmish come to be known as the Battle of the Plains of Abraham? The answer is really pretty straightforward and even quite typically Canadian. The fight occurred on land owned by a farmer named Abraham Martin.

EXPULSION OF THE ACADIANS

LET'S HEAR YOU SWEAR. In a masterful example of military thinking, the English decided that the residents of Acadia (an area including parts of present-day Nova Scotia, New Brunswick and Prince Edward Island) were a threat. The folks had lived there peacefully for years, but that didn't seem to matter. The Acadians suddenly had a choice. Either swear allegiance to England or be gone.

OUT YOU GO. When they refused to swear allegiance, the British rounded up the Acadians and, in 1755, shipped them off.

A PRETTY FICTION. At some point we've probably all been exposed to Longfellow's loooong poem "Evangeline." The dreadfully sad and, frankly, syrupy poem is based on the expulsion of the Acadians. It gives the impression that the people meekly submitted to being thrown off their land. Was that the case? You have a negative on that.

ACADIA'S LOUIS RIEL. Present-day Acadians, many of whom live in Louisiana, dug back 250 years. And when they did, they discovered a hero. Joseph Broussard had organized a resistance movement. He and his patriots fought the expulsion every way they could. When the English threw them in jail, their wives smuggled cutlery to the prisoners, who escaped by digging their way out with spoons!

PINING FOR THE HOMELAND. By 1765, Broussard and his companions were forced to give up their battle. He led a group of about 200 Acadians, and together they sailed away from their homeland. Broussard himself did not live long after arriving in Louisiana, but his descendants haven't let the story of his heroism die.

DIG THIS. In honour of the 250th anniversary of the expulsion, there are plans to dig up Broussard's remains and bring them to Canada. Well, that's one way to thank a guy, I guess.

WHAT A SWEET GIRL THAT LAURA WAS

*The War of 1812 was such a Canadian sort of a war,
even though Canada as we know it today didn't exist at the time
it was fought. The war is only part of our history because the
Americans and the British decided to work out their differences
on our land. By the time the fighting was all over,
Canada's boundaries had pretty much been settled and an
otherwise ordinary woman had become a hero.*

GUESS WHO'S COMING TO DINNER? On June 21, 1813, the
Secord family had some unexpected (and uninvited!) company
for dinner—a group of enemy soldiers from the United States.
After a big meal accompanied by liberal doses of liquid refresh-
ment, the Secord's American dinner guests were relaxed enough
to talk a bit about their immediate future. It seemed that the
American military was planning a surprise attack at a place not
too far from the Secords' home.

THE WALLS HAVE EARS. Mrs. Secord, Laura to those who knew
her well, listened carefully as her well-fed and slightly tipsy
intruders talked on. The men bragged that 500 soldiers were
marching towards Lieutenant James FitzGibbon's post at Beaver
Dams even as they spoke—and drank.

SURPRISE! FitzGibbon, they were sure, would be unprepared for
the onslaught, and the Americans would gain ground—Canadian
ground, that is—permanently. It didn't take Laura long to decide
what she had to do. The woman was up and out of the house
before dawn the next day. She needed to get to Beaver Dams
before the American soldiers did.

AN EARLY MORNING CONSTITUTIONAL. The shortest route would have been the easiest one for Laura Secord, but it would have meant taking the roads. She was afraid that she'd be stopped by American guards along the way, so she took a route through the woods. It was almost twice as long and, of course, held its own dangers, but there was less chance of the enemy seeing her.

THE MARATHON CONTINUES. Night had fallen, and Laura Secord had walked more than 30 kilometres by the time she arrived at Beaver Dams. Her gruelling journey was worth it though. She reached Lieutenant FitzGibbon in time to ruin the "surprise" part of the surprise attack the Americans had planned. And in doing that she pretty much ruined the "attack" part of the plan too.

NO, REALLY, IT ONLY LOOKS LIKE 50 MEN. A party of Six Nations warriors who were friendly with Britain headed the Americans off before they reached the British post. FitzGibbon, who must have been blessed with a fine gift of the gab, convinced the enemy that he had a lean, mean fighting machine just waiting to pounce, and his men never had to fire a shot.

GOODBYE FOR NOW. The Americans retreated. The British had not one casualty. Better still, the Battle of Beaver Dams was a turning point in the War of 1812. And Laura Secord was its unlikely hero.

SHHH. For years the Secords were secretive about Laura's historic role. They didn't want to tempt the fates—or the Americans—and risk retaliation. As the years passed, though, the threat became less and the story of Laura Secord's amazing journey became public.

IN APPRECIATION. England's Prince of Wales rewarded Laura's determination and bravery with a gift of gold. Since her death (at the ripe old age of 93) in 1868, our hero of the War of 1812 has been immortalized in songs, poetry, books and plays.

THE LEGEND GROWS. In his romantic version of Laura Secord's adventure, author William F. Coffin added a cow to the story! He had her herding a cow as a ruse in case anyone saw her traipsing through the woods. She didn't have a cow.

THERE'S SOMETHING ABOUT LAURA. She would never have made it if she'd had anything more to care for than her own two, sore feet. But Coffin wasn't one to place too much emphasis on the truth anyway. He even had our hero's name wrong. He referred to her as Mary instead of Laura.

NO CHOCOLATES EITHER? One hundred years later, a candy manufacturer decided that Laura Secord's image would be a good marketing tool. It seems he was correct in that assumption, for Laura Secord chocolates are still very popular with Canadians.

IS NOTHING SACRED? Unfortunately, in an ironic twist the Laura Secord candy company is now owned by an American corporation. Poor Laura, she must be rolling in her grave!

TIT FOR TAT. But the war did not end there. By the following summer the two sides were still at it. American troops had set fire to a good-sized chunk of Toronto, including government buildings. They even stole our parliamentary mace. Now *that* was a low blow, one that pretty much demanded retaliation.

OUR TURN TO FIGHT DIRTY. The Canadians waited patiently to get back at the Americans. Their chance came in August 1814. Our troops stormed Washington, DC. The Americans were caught totally unaware. They fled from their own capital while Canadian and British troops acted in a most impolite fashion by trashing the city—and setting fire to the White House.

EVERLASTING EFFECT. The presidential residence was gutted. The Americans rebuilt it as quickly as possible. This included a quick whitewashing of the exterior, which is one of the reasons it's called the White House.

FORGET ME NOT. One small section of a wall in the White House was not repaired after that devastating fire. Every president of the United States since then has had to pass a burned spot in a doorway. That scorch mark was left there purposely as a not-so-subtle reminder of vulnerability.

DID YOU  KNOW?

ONE SORCERER, NO APPRENTICE. Jean Pierre Lavallee was well known in his neighbourhood on the Island of Orleans near Québec City. In this case, though, the phrase "well known" shouldn't be confused with "well liked." Lavallee was a sorcerer. In 1711, he conjured up fogs so thick that eight British ships ran aground on rocks.

SECRETS OF THE FALLS

Psssst, wanna buy some trinkets from the War of 1812?
Well, sorry, you're too late.
They were all snatched up late in March—
March of 1848, that is.

THE SILENCE WAS DEAFENING. On the night of March 29, 1848, the folks living around Niagara Falls suddenly realized that they were hearing a very strange sound. They almost didn't recognize the sound because, what with living near the noisy falls and all, they'd rarely heard it. It was the sound of silence. The falls had stopped running.

WHAT A CREEPY SCENE. People left their homes, and even their beds, to investigate this strange situation. By the next morning, thousands of curious onlookers from kilometres around had arrived to see the history-making phenomenon for themselves. The river bed and the falls were dry. Fish lay dead and dying.

LET'S GO, KIDS. Youngsters scrambled around, exploring caves on the river bottom. Souvenir hunters picked through dozens of bayonets, muskets, swords, gun barrels and even tomahawks that had been hidden by the deep river waters since the War of 1812.

WHY DID THE CURIOUS CROSS THE RIVER? Because they could. On March 30, 1848, some folks walked across the river while others rode horses. Of course, it wouldn't be Niagara Falls without hawkers to take advantage of a naturally occurring situation. The water was gone, but the hucksters certainly weren't, and you could hire a horse and buggy for a ride to the other side of the river.

OH LORD! But not everyone was taking this extraordinary event lightly. Many people were terrified that Niagara Falls running dry was an omen of dreadful things to come. Local ministers conducted special church services to offer assurance to the superstitious. Those with a more practical bent got busy blasting out rocks that had been navigational hazards.

ANOTHER LOST OPPORTUNITY. Thirty hours after the falls had stopped, a great wall of water rushed towards the precipice. Things were normal again and have stayed that way ever since. Chances of the Canadian Falls stopping again are pretty slim. Hate to tell you, but this might mean we've already collected all the artifacts from the War of 1812 that we'll ever have.

BUT WHY? Of course it wasn't the end of the world that had stopped the falls from falling. It was just an ice jam on Lake Erie that had caused all the commotion—or lack of it.

DID YOU  KNOW?

HOW'D THAT HAPPEN? In the early 1800s, the British ship *Wave* sank off the Gaspe Peninsula's east coast. In the early 1900s, *Wave*'s anchor was hauled out of Lake Ontario's Hamilton Bay, more than 2200 kilometres from where it sank.

OUR FOUNDING FATHERS

*The Fathers of Confederation created the beginnings
of the country we know and love today. Thanks, Dad(s)!*

WHAT'S IN A NAME? He was born in Nova Scotia, became British Columbia's second premier and was influential in bringing that western province into Confederation. Bill Smith must've been quite the fellow, because he changed his name to Amor De Cosmos—which means "Lover of the Universe."

WHAT'S IN THE SAME NAME? When you read about the meetings that the Fathers of Confederation held, you just might get the impression that John Hamilton Gray was a very busy boy. That's because there wasn't just one man named John Hamilton Gray, but two! Two of the 36 Fathers of Confederation had exactly the same name.

AN AMERICAN? Yes, William P. Howland, one of our founding fathers, was an American!

THEY DIDN'T DO IT FOR THE MONEY. In 1867, Canada's politicians earned the princely sum of $6.00 a day!

PARTY ON, DUDES! Québécois Fathers of Confederation brought their Mothers—okay, not really *their* mothers, but the mothers of their children. The presence of the women offered the perfect excuse to party hearty after a tough day at the bargaining table.

MEETINGS IN TRIPLICATE. Charlottetown is known as the Cradle of Confederation, but there were actually three conferences, and it is the Québec conference of 1864 that is depicted in the painting every school kid is familiar with. There was also a conference held in England.

WHATEVER. The Fathers of Confederation met in Charlotteown because the delegates from Prince Edward Island didn't care enough about becoming part of Canada to leave their little island.

BOYS WILL BE BOYS. Two Fathers of Confederation, Sir John A. Macdonald and George Brown, actively disliked each other. They managed to put their differences aside during that trip to England. They found peashooters and fired tiny projectiles into a crowd attending a horse race—a crowd that included Queen Victoria!

QUEEN VICTORIA OFFERS HER OPINION. England's leader once called John A. Macdonald, Canada's first prime minister, "an interesting and agreeable old man." She likely missed the time that he was so drunk he had to hang onto his desk in order to keep himself upright. And she must not have known that he once threw up on stage, because after Confederation she knighted him!

THE KINGDOM OF CANADA? New Brunswick's Leonard Tilley didn't invent the famous hat that bears his name, but in 1866 he suggested that Canada be referred to as a "dominion" rather than a "kingdom." He thought it best not to risk offending the Americans who had, just the century before, severed their ties with both British and French royalty.

THIS WORKS BETTER. The word "dominion" comes from a Biblical passage (Psalm 72) that reads in part, "He shall have dominion also from sea to sea." An apt choice considering Canada stretches "from sea to sea."

ALL IN THE FAMILY. Father of Confederation George-Étienne Cartier was a descendent of Jacques Cartier. For reasons likely unconnected to his family lineage, George, as he preferred to be called, wore a miniature image of Napoleon on a chain around his neck.

WHY OTTAWA? After much debate, and probably a few committees struck, Queen Victoria decreed that the lumber town of Ottawa would be Canada's capital city. Her reasoning was that both French- and English-speaking folk lived there, and that it wouldn't be hard to defend if the Americans attacked. There are probably worse reasons for choosing the location of a capital city.

MONDAY'S CHILD IS FAIR OF FACE. July 1, 1867, Canada's birthday, was a Monday.

DID YOU KNOW?

GET IN LINE. We all know that the province of Québec has threatened to separate from the rest of Canada. Then some extremists in Alberta thought that the West should go its own way. But did you know that the first separatists were from Nova Scotia? Canada was only months old when Nova Scotians elected an Anti-Confederation Party to power. Fortunately, the strange party's leader, William Annand, well, failed to lead. And the rest, as they say, is history.

THEY STAND ON GUARD FOR US

*Canada has the rather odd distinction of being known
for its national police force.
The red serge uniform of the Royal Canadian Mounted Police
is recognized worldwide. For most of our country's history,
the Mounties have generally been a source of great pride.*

HOW IT ALL BEGAN. In 1873, our esteemed leader, Prime
Minister Sir John A. Macdonald, decided that settlers heading
to western Canada would have a better chance of successfully
settling if there was a police force to "maintain the right." The
North-West Mounted Police force was formed to do exactly that.

ROLE MODELS. The new force was modelled on the unlikely
combination of the Royal Irish Constabulary and the American
cavalry.

WHAT'S IN A NAME? Francis Jeffrey Dickens was one of the
original members of the North-West Mounted Police. His father's
name might be more familiar to you—Charles Dickens. Poor
Jeffrey, as he was known, probably left England and came to
Canada because he was suffering from "middle child syndrome."
He was the fifth of Dickens' 10 children and, rumour had it,
didn't exactly distinguish himself as a police officer.

ROYALLY POLICED. In 1904, the official name of the force became
the Royal North-West Mounted Police. In 1920, that force
merged with the Dominion Police, and ever since, Canadians
have been proud of their Mounties—the Royal Canadian
Mounted Police.

SQUEAKY CLEAN—ALMOST. Sadly, Canada's national police force has been known to make history by breaking the law. In 1977, a Royal Commission determined that the Mounties had stepped way over the line by spying on certain Canadians. Their sins were serious, and the RCMP's spy squad was disbanded.

HOW MICKEY MOUSE WAS THAT? In 1995, amid great Canadian indignation, the Mounties handed over control of their image on souvenirs and collectibles to the very American Disney Corporation. Bad feelings and equally bad jokes flew from sea to sea. What could we expect next, mouse ears on the proud stetsons? Fortunately, the five-year contract between Canada's finest and the Mickey Mouse company expired. Worst-case scenarios had not come true.

NO COP FORCE LIKE AN OLD COP FORCE. As old as it is, the RCMP is not the oldest police force in Canada. That honour belongs to a different force with similar initials—RNC—and not nearly the recognition factor. By the time the British and the French were duking it out on the Plains of Abraham, the Royal Newfoundland Constabulary was 30 years old!

THOSE WERE THE DAYS. Before Newfoundland joined Confederation in 1949, the RNC was known as the National Police Force of the Dominion of Newfoundland. Pretty impressive name. Too bad the cops who made up the elaborately named force were not treated so well. By 1969 the highest-paid constable with the RNC earned a princely *(not!)* $440 a month, making them the lowest-paid cops in Canada—by far.

IT GETS WORSE. These underpaid policemen (there were no women on the force in those days) had no way of bargaining to improve their lot. And so, in September 1969, a committee of constables met with the police chief to see if things could be improved.

AND WORSE STILL. Over the next few months the situation became considerably more tense. Soon Premier Joey Smallwood waded into the fray and threatened to disband the entire police force. The cops didn't blink. They knew that the public was on their side and they, in turn, threatened to strike.

LAW-BREAKING POLICE. But because they had no collective agreement, the strike was illegal. This meant that the whole police force was about to break the law they were supposed to be enforcing. Things were definitely getting out of hand. The only folks who were happy about the situation were the Newfoundland journalists assigned to headline writing. They certainly didn't have to look far to come up with colour!

ALL'S WELL THAT ENDS WELL. Finally Premier Smallwood backed down. The police chief, who had *not* sided with his men, resigned. The cops formed a Brotherhood that still functions— very effectively—to this day. It welcomed its first female "brother" to the "hood" on December 15, 1980.

THE FAMOUS FIVE

POP QUIZ. (Or should that be Mom Quiz?) Oops, didn't we mention that there'd be a test? Oh well, sorry about that, but we're sure you'll do just fine.

1. Who were the Famous Five?
A) Canadian car manufacturers?
B) The number of Fathers of Confederation who were sober at the signing?
C) Emily Murphy, Henrietta Edwards, Nellie McClung, Louise McKinney and Irene Parlby, the five women who fought to have Canadian women recognized as "persons."
D) All of the above.

If you chose A), B) or D), please check for a pulse.

2. Emily Murphy ...
A) had energy and ambition to spare, was a police magistrate, a social reformer and lusted after an appointment to the Senate.
B) enjoyed dancing in her nightie.
C) had four friends with similar interests.
D) all of the above.

If you chose D), give yourself as many points as you like. Be generous. These points are worth about as much as a woman's political opinion prior to 1929.

3. What did Emily Murphy do with all of this?
Well, finally, a question with some meat to it. Let's make that the end of the quiz. You no doubt did extraordinarily well, so just relax and read on.

WE'D LIKE TO HELP YOU, MA'AM, BUT YOU'RE NOT A PERSON.
Now Ms Murphy was not a woman who enjoyed rejection.
When she was turned down for that Senate appointment, she
was, frankly, pretty miffed—especially when she heard the reason she'd been told "no." The Canadian government would not
appoint Emily Murphy to the Senate because she wasn't a "person"
according to the British North America Act.

WHO YA GONNA CALL? Murphy was infuriated. She called on
four of her closest friends, who all just happened to share Murphy's
ambitions, energy level and opinions on social reform. Together
they approached the Supreme Court of Canada. In the spring of
1928, the court made it official. Women were not "persons." Emily
Murphy (and her compatriots) had been told "no" once again.

WE'RE NOT GOING TO TAKE IT. Outraged, the five women
approached Britain's Privy Council, which was the court of final
appeal for Canada at the time. On October 18, 1929, the
Council ruled, "The exclusion of women from all public offices
is a relic of days more barbarous than ours." Emily declared,
"We won! We won!" and danced about in her nightie.
(Fortunately, she was at home when she heard the news!)

GOOD NEWS, BAD NEWS. The Privy Council ruling was definitely a great victory for women. But the fact that England's
court could—and did—overturn a decision made by Canada's
highest court wasn't such great news for Canada's independence
as a nation.

MUCH WORSE NEWS. Eleven days later, the New York stock
market crashed, heralding the beginning of the Great Depression.
There's no connection between the two events, but the timing
did mean that people's attention shifted from women's rights
and constitutional independence to mere survival.

SOME THINGS CAN TAKE WAY MORE TIME. The Famous Five had not fought their battle for every woman—or even every man—in the country. Canada's 1880 Indian Act, for instance, defined "person" as "an individual other than an Indian." It took just the tiniest bit longer to rectify *that* situation. Native people in Canada couldn't vote in national elections until 1960!

AND WHAT OF THE COLONY'S INDEPENDENCE? Well, that took even longer yet. By the 1980s, the British North America Act was still in effect. Now, the BNA Act was probably a fine and useful document when it was drafted by John A. Macdonald and his colleagues—in 1867. But for goodness' sake, times had changed.

FREE AT LAST! Finally, on April 17, 1982, Prime Minister Pierre Trudeau sat down at a table across from Queen Elizabeth II. Together they signed the necessary paper to make Canada an independent nation—sort of. And then it began to rain—which wouldn't have been so bad except that this signing took place outside.

WELL, AT LEAST A LITTLE FREER. And so, 115 years after Confederation, we finally had our independence—except that the British monarch is still our official head of state. Oh well, can't win 'em all.

THE FLAG

QUICK QUESTION. Why have Canadians never been flag wavers to the extent Americans are?

ANSWER. Probably because Canada didn't really have a flag until 98 years after it became a country.

BUT WHY? Well, some things just take a bit of time.

MIKE'S MANDATE. Yes, inexcusable as it was, Canada's own flag didn't fly until February 15, 1965. There had been attempts to get the wheels in motion before, but, frankly, they had not been very determined efforts. It wasn't until Prime Minister Lester B. Pearson—"Mike" to those who knew him best—pointed out in Parliament that it was ridiculous not to have a national flag that things really began to roll.

MADLY OFF IN ALL DIRECTIONS. Surely having our very own flag would create a united pride. No such luck! The great flag debate splintered Canadian unity. Some people wanted to stay with the two borrowed flags we were already using—the Union Jack and the Red Ensign. Others wanted a new design, but there wasn't much agreement on which new design. Oh my.

HOW ABOUT A COLLAGE? John Diefenbaker, leader of the opposition, declared that the Union Jack must be somewhere on the new flag. That was a nod to our British heritage, he said. The French wanted the fleur-de-lis. But by this time there were hundreds of thousands of Canadian citizens with no connection to either France or England, so neither of those symbols meant anything to them.

WHEN ALL ELSE FAILS, STRIKE A COMMITTEE. The new flag committee was certainly popular with Canadians. Over 2000 different design ideas were proposed!

STOP! It seemed as though the debate could have gone on forever. Finally, in the early hours of December 15, 1964, Pearson put his official foot down. He ended the debate by using Parliamentary rules of closure.

SING IT OUT. Then the Liberals stood and sang an impromptu rendition of "O Canada." In response, the Conservatives gave a rousing performance of "God Save the Queen." And Canada finally had a flag to call its own—the stylized red maple leaf, bordered by two red bars and designed by George H.G. Stanley.

WHEW! IT'S OVER! Pearson was pleased. He'd created a legacy for his term as prime minister. The opposition leader, John Diefenbaker, was apoplectic. Everyone else was just exhausted and had to go to the bathroom.

THAT'S NOT THE FLAG WE FOUGHT FOR. During this time, wherever Pearson happened to be, he took the opportunity to promote the new flag as a positive and important step in our country's development as a nation. A diplomat at heart, Pearson always chose his words to suit his audience. Despite this, he was loudly and repeatedly booed when he spoke to a Royal Canadian Legion meeting in Winnipeg.

THANKS, EH? But Pearson persevered, and on February 15, 1965, Canada's flag was raised on Parliament Hill for the very first time. It only stayed there for a few days before being replaced by a duplicate. The original was handed to Lucien Lamoureux, the deputy speaker of the House of Commons, as a reward for his support.

WHERE'D IT GO? Lamoureux retired from politics, became a diplomat, moved to Brussels, Belgium, and took the keepsake flag with him. He died in 1998. His widow, Elisabeth Hoffmann-Lamoureux kept the flag—even after she was asked to give it back. Finally, in the spring of 2005, after "no particular negotiations," a Canadian diplomat flew to Belgium, received the flag from Mme. Hoffmann-Lamoureux, and our piece of history came home.

SIMPLE BUT EFFECTIVE. By now it's difficult to imagine Canada as a nation without our distinctive symbol. That unique red leaf is so popular and easily identified around the world that even people who are not Canadian sew the emblem on some part of their clothing when they are travelling. It's a small, subtle but very effective statement, one that people are proud to be associated with.

WRAPPING HIMSELF IN BOTH FLAGS. Of course, there's always an exception. When John Diefenbaker died in 1979, 14 years after the flag issue had been settled, both the "new" Canadian flag *and* the Red Ensign lay across his coffin.

WHAT GALL!

HAPPY HUNDREDTH, CANADA. In 1967, Canada celebrated its 100th birthday. Feelings of pride and patriotism ran high throughout the country. There were parties and special projects in virtually every Canadian community. The biggest party, though, was held in Montréal—Expo 67. And what a great time it was. A total success. People from all over the world came and admired our accomplishments.

COME ON DOWN! We invited royalty, celebrities and heads of state to join in the big bash. Dozens of them accepted our invitation to the birthday party. They enjoyed themselves. And behaved themselves. All, that is, except France's president, Charles de Gaulle.

WAY TO GO, CHUCK! If there was a prize for the most inappropriate comment made on Canadian soil, it would have to go to de Gaulle. Upon his arrival in Montréal, he made a stirring speech. He started by comparing that city to Paris after the Nazi occupation. He ended by shouting, "Vive le Montréal! Vive le Québec! Vive le Québec libre!" He was calling Québec separatists to arms.

HE'S OUTA HERE. Even the usual Canadian politeness could not overlook such rudeness. He had accepted our hospitality and then proceeded to insult us and try to damage us. Prime Minister Lester Pearson reacted strongly. He called de Gaulle's words "unacceptable." A few days later the disgraced French leader left Canada.

BAD STUFF. But damage had already been done. There were cells of revolutionaries operating in Québec. The idea of separation was growing. A terrorist group calling itself the Front de libération du Québec formed. Over the next few years it made itself a focus of attention by committing a variety of crimes, including bombings and armed robberies.

TOTALLY OUT OF HAND. On October 5, 1970, the FLQ's criminal activities became an international problem. FLQ members kidnapped James Cross, Britain's trade commissioner to Canada. Their letter of demand for Cross's release ended by quoting Charles de Gaulle—"Vive le Québec libre!" Five days later the FLQ also kidnapped Québec cabinet minister Pierre Laporte. The terrorists had accomplished one of their main goals. Canadians were, indeed, terrified.

TAKING TOTAL CONTROL. Prime Minister Pierre Trudeau reacted swiftly and surely. He invoked the War Measures Act and ordered the army to patrol the streets of Ottawa, Montréal and Québec City. Now Canadians had more than just the FLQ to fear. How far would Trudeau go? they wondered. The angered and arrogant leader retorted with a memorable quote of his own, "Just watch me!"

NEVER AGAIN. Peace eventually prevailed, but it came too late for Pierre Laporte. His body was discovered in the trunk of an abandoned car. His murderers were caught, tried and jailed. James Cross was freed. The FLQ became history. So did Charles de Gaulle's visit to Canada.

O CANADA!

IT WOULD'VE BEEN TOO PERFECT. Popular legend has it that Calixa Lavallée, who wrote the music for our national anthem, was an obscure composer who "just happened" to write the piece. That's an awfully good story—certainly a far better story than the actual truth.

A JOB FOR A TRAINED PROFESSIONAL. Lavallée was an accomplished composer who had written symphonies, operettas and various other pieces of music. He was considered Canada's "national composer." In 1880, he was commissioned to write the piece we know as "O Canada."

MOVING RIGHT ALONG. The anthem was first performed on June 24, 1880, in Québec City. And only 100 years later, it officially became our national anthem.

DIG THAT COMPOSER. Lavallée died in 1891 at the age of 49. He was buried near Boston, but Canadians didn't think that was an appropriate final resting place for the man who wrote our anthem. So we dug him up, shipped him across the border and reburied him in 1933.

THEY'RE SINGING OUR SONG. Adolphe-Basile Routhier, a Québec judge, penned the French lyrics to "O Canada." For some reason those words weren't translated into the other official language. Instead, there were several sets of English lyrics to "O Canada." In 1908, another Québec judge, Robert Weir, wrote the words that became the basis for the anthem English Canadians sing today.

CANADIAN CONTRIBUTIONS

*Canadians have made some important
contributions to world arts, letters and history.
Some were good contributions; others were, well...*

LEGENDS OF THE SILVER SCREEN

A LAUGH A MINUTE! We've all seen clips from the old Keystone Kops' slapstick comedies, with the hapless police chasing bad guys. You watch the jerky movement flicker across the screen, knowing that at some point someone will throw a pie. But did you know that Mack Sennett, who made those movies, was a Canadian? The pie-in-the-face shtick that became his trademark wasn't his idea, but it too was Canadian.

THE ORIGINAL SIN? Sennett's friend Doc Kelley was a travelling medicine man. In 1889, Kelley was touring Newfoundland, hustling his snake oil, when he happened to catch a bit of street theatre. It seems that as he and a bunch of other men stood at the side of the road and watched, the hotel's cook came tearing along, chasing a young stable hand away from a hotel.

TAKE THIS! The boy had put a fair chunk of real estate between himself and his pursuer when he stopped, turned around and tried to reason with the cook. His attempt at diplomacy failed miserably. The cook had apparently been carrying a piece of pie, and in exasperation he threw it at the lad. It hit the boy's chest and left a big stain on his shirt.

THERE'S GOLD IN THAT STORY, BOY. Kelley's background as a travelling medical man no doubt gave him some insight into what attracted people's attention. He realized that incident had a nugget of potential. By exaggerating the scene he had just witnessed and introducing it to Mack Sennett, Doc Kelley unwittingly gave birth to an entire film genre.

FROM COLLECTING JUNK TO MAKING MOVIES. The piston that drove Hollywood's MGM grew up in Canada. Louis B. Mayer's father was a junk dealer in St. John, New Brunswick.

ABLE TO LEAP TALL BUILDINGS! In 1934, while the Great Depression raged around him, a 17-year-old Canadian, Joe Shuster, created the comic-book hero Superman. Shuster modelled the imaginary gangster-ridden city Metropolis on his hometown of Toronto. The *Daily Planet,* where Clark Kent, Superman's alter ego, worked as a reporter, was based on the *Toronto Daily Star* newspaper.

EVERYONE LOVES THE GUY WITH THE CAPE. By the 1940s the Superman comic books were so popular that the Man of Steel had also become a radio show. By the 1950s, it was a television show.

HOW CANADIAN. Sadly, by that time Joe Shuster, Superman's Canadian creator, had sold control of his superhero to an American comic book publisher. If you think that's awful, read on. The selling price was $130! Some years later Shuster sued the company—unsuccessfully. By 1975, the man who had thought up Superman's X-ray vision was nearly blind. And he was destitute.

SUPER MOVIE. The first Superman movie, made in 1978, continued the Canadian connection. The film was shot in High River, Alberta. Québec-born Glen Ford played Clark Kent's adoptive father, and Canadian actress Margot Kidder played Lois Lane.

BUT WHAT OF SHUSTER? American media giant Warner Communications, by then owner of the rights to Superman's image, learned of Joe Shuster's great hardship. They granted the hero's originator a stipend of $20,000 annually, which the artist collected until he died in 1992, at the age of 78.

MORE MOVIES. The Canadian movie *Porkys,* shot in 1981, made a pork-barrel full of money (it's still the largest grossing movie in Canadian history), spawned two sequels and created a new genre of film—the grossout movie.

WIN SOME, LOSE SOME. The critically acclaimed movie *Days of Heaven* was shot in 1978 at Whisky Gap, Alberta. Maybe the town's less-than-sober-sounding name should have been a warning because that film is also something of a record holder. It lost more money than almost any movie ever filmed anywhere.

YOU CAN'T EAT FAME. The first-ever feature-length documentary movie was made in the early 1920s. Alakarialak, an Inuit man from Inukjuak, became famous as one of the "stars" of *Nanook of the North.* A lot of good it did him—he died of starvation in 1923.

THE ULTIMATE OPENING NIGHT. By the afternoon of November 14, 1606, the stage was set. The first non-Native play ever performed in Canada was set to go. Samuel de Champlain had just returned to New France, and in honour of the occasion, the boys put on the play that Marc Lescarbot had spent the previous winter writing.

THE PLAY'S THE THING. In case you missed it, the play was called *Le Theatre de Neptune en la Nouvelle France.* Hopefully Champlain enjoyed his evening's entertainment.

THE GREAT CANADIAN APPLE MYSTERY

HOW IT ALL BEGAN. It was springtime, 1811, in Upper Canada. A farmer named John McIntosh was hard at work clearing his land. As he chopped and cleared, McIntosh was delighted to notice a few tiny apple tree saplings poking out of the soil. What a treat an apple would be in the winter, he must have thought as he carefully transplanted the seedlings to a spot where they'd grow better.

BUT IT DIDN'T WORK. By the following year, all but one of the transplanted apple trees had died. Even so, McIntosh could not have considered his experiment a failure because the fruit from the one surviving tree was delicious.

EVERYONE WANTS A BITE. People liked the crisp, tart taste of John's new apples so much that McIntosh wanted an orchard full of these trees.

BUT IT DIDN'T WORK—TAKE TWO! Call it a quirk of nature, but no matter how many trees he planted using the seeds from those apples, none of them would produce exactly the same fruit that the first one had. McIntosh had all but given up trying when an itinerant worker happened along to the door of his farmhouse.

AND THEN... The family welcomed the man's offer of help. Little did they know that the decision to hire this particular worker would change the course of agricultural history.

GRAFT IS GOOD. Try grafting a branch from the successful tree onto another apple tree seedling, the hired man suggested. All summer long, John McIntosh, his son Allan and the anonymous wandering worker toiled away grafting stocks.

MYSTERIOUS SUCCESS. Their efforts were rewarded. Today the McIntosh apple is grown all over the world and is the most popular of all varieties of the fruit. But this Canadian success story leaves a mystery in its wake.

HOW'D IT HAPPEN? If the McIntosh apple tree is self-sterile and the only way to produce an actual McIntosh apple is to graft a McIntosh shoot onto another variety of apple tree, then how did the first seedling tree that John transplanted in 1811 come to exist?

SOMETIMES YOU JUST GET LUCKY. The only possible answer to that mystery is simply fortunate coincidence. Someone, some years before, must have been munching on an apple while walking across the land that became the McIntosh farm, The hungry traveller must have tossed his or her apple core at exactly the spot where it cross-pollinated with another tree and produced the seedlings McIntosh transplanted.

A STRANGE LEGACY. That original McIntosh apple tree died in 1910. A small monument marks the spot where it grew, and a computer now carries its name. It seems that super-geek Steve Jobs loves apples. As something of a joke, in 1976, Jobs and his partners registered their upstart company as Apple Computers Incorporated.

WHAT'S IN A NAME? Five years later, an employee of Apple Computers created a small, easy-to-use personal computer, which he then (sensibly) named after his favourite kind of apple. He mistakenly spelled the name Macintosh, but it's doubtful that John McIntosh would have minded!

TELE—AND OTHER— COMMUNICATIONS

TRANS-ATLANTIC MESSAGE. In 1901, Guglielmo Marconi received the first-ever trans-Atlantic wireless message. He only managed to pick up the letter "S," but it was a start. Not surprisingly, the place in Newfoundland where he was stationed when the "message" came through is now known as Signal Hill.

HE'S OURS! NO, HE'S OURS! The Americans claim that the telephone was their invention. The Scots claim it was theirs, and in Canada, well, we think we rang first. The controversy stems from the debate over the nationality of the telephone's inventor. Alexander Graham Bell cared very much more about scientific discovery than he did about credit or even national boundaries.

FIRST EMERGENCY PHONE CALL. On March 12, 1875, Bell was working alone in his lab. While reaching for something, he spilled some acid on himself. Thomas Watson, Bell's assistant, was working in the next room. There were rudimentary versions of Bell's latest invention in both rooms. With the acid burning his skin, Bell called out for help. The mouthpiece of his first-generation telephone picked up the sound of Bell's voice.

HELP ARRIVES. Watson ran to Bell's side—not to help the injured man, but to let him know that their years of hard work had finally paid off. The telephone had officially been invented.

LET'S MAKE IT OFFICIAL. On Valentine's Day in 1876, Alexander Graham Bell registered a patent on his amazing device that could transmit the human voice from one room to another. In a strange twist of science known as simultaneous discovery, an American scientist, Elisha Gray, approached the same patent office to register essentially the same device not two hours after Bell did.

DR. FRANKENSTEIN'S MONSTER? Later in his life, Bell took to wrapping his phone in cloth so that he couldn't hear it ring. He once said, "I never use the beast." It makes you wonder what he'd think if he could see all of us going about our lives with cellphones plastered to the sides of our heads!

MA BELL TOO. Alexander Graham had clearly inherited an inventive mind. Bell's mother was profoundly deaf, and both his father and grandfather had devoted their lives to finding ways to help deaf people communicate. Meanwhile, Bell's wife worked on the development of independent flight.

THOSE CRAZY YOUNG MEN IN THEIR FLYING MACHINES. Alexander Graham Bell's work didn't stop there. He registered over 100 patents, many of which, like the iron lung, changed the course of history. Bell was living in his beloved Baddeck, Nova Scotia, when he and Canada's first pilot, John McCurdy, managed to get their plane, the Silver Dart, to fly.

MAKING IT FROM SCRATCH. In April 1974, Canada's National Research Council took on the challenge of developing a robotic arm that would work in space! Every nut, every bolt, every concept of this project was new.

UP, UP AND AWAY. Seven years later the robotic Canadarm flew into space on board the Columbia. The arm worked exactly the way it was intended to work—as an arm, an extension of the human body. It even resembled a human arm—if a human arm were 15 metres in length and weighed 410 kilograms!

NEW AND IMPROVED. In April 2001, Canadarm 2 was launched aboard *Endeavour* en route to the International Space Station, where it was installed to help construct the station. Before this "bigger, smarter and more grown-up" arm dug into its work, the original Canadarm and the newest addition to the family enjoyed a symbolic handshake—in space, of course.

UNDERGROUND TO FREEDOM

*The Underground Railroad only operated for 20 years,
but it dramatically changed the course of history
in Canada and in the United States.*

THIS TRAIN IS BOUND FOR GLORY. Britain abolished slavery throughout its empire, including Canada, in 1833. It didn't take long for the slaves in America to hear about this free land to the north. Many were anxious to try to escape from slavery—at any cost and in any way they could. Josiah Henson was one of the first of those slaves.

AN INSPIRATIONAL JOURNEY. With his wife, four children, a bit of food and the small sum of 25 cents, Henson ran from his owner's property in Kentucky. He made it to southern Ontario, where he and his family settled. Henson was so loyal to Canada that he fought in the 1837 Rebellion. It's said that he was the inspiration for the title character in Harriet Beecher Stowe's book *Uncle Tom's Cabin*.

CRIMINALS FOR THE GREATER GOOD. By 1850, so many slaves had run away from their owners that the United States Congress made it illegal for anyone to hide or help a runaway slave. Anyone caught helping a slave would be arrested, charged and heavily fined—even if they lived in a free state. The person the United States government most wanted to catch was Harriet Tubman.

SUPERHUMAN DETERMINATION. Tubman had been born a slave. Her owner had once beaten her so badly that he fractured her skull, but he had clearly not broken her spirit. She escaped from the south, and working from her new home in St. Catharines,

Ontario, she made trip after dangerous trip across the border and into the southern states.

HUGE BOUNTY. Over a period of seven years Tubman rescued hundreds of slaves and brought them safely to Canada. The price on her head was an astounding $40,000—a veritable king's ransom in those days.

RIDING THE RAILS. Tubman and others formed the Underground Railroad, a loosely knit organization of brave people willing to defy the unjust laws and help the slaves to freedom. From 1840 to 1860, it's thought that as many as 30,000 travelled that "railroad" to Canada.

DID YOU  KNOW?

WAIT FOR THE BUS. Did you know that Charlottetown, Prince Edward Island, the cradle of Canadian Confederation, did not have public transit until October 2005?

AHEAD OF HIS TIME

Progress can certainly bring its own set of problems.
Fortunately, solving those problems
is a way of progressing even further.

MOVING RIGHT ALONG. Once the last spike had been driven into the Canadian Pacific Railway, Canadians could travel from sea to sea, or even from town to town, much more quickly than ever before.

WILL THE TRAIN BE ON TIME? Believe it or not, being able to travel farther and faster actually created a problem for Canadians—and certainly for Canadian railroads. You see, in most of the world, Canada included, each community determined its own time by declaring that it was noon when the sun was exactly overhead. This made train scheduling extremely difficult.

IN THE ZONE...BUT WHICH ONE? Railroad operators decided they would solve the problem by creating their own zones. That might have worked, except there were several different railroad companies and they all used a slightly different system.

A MAN OF HIS TIME. Sandford Fleming came to Canada from Scotland during 1845. He was a surveyor, an engineer and a bit of a darling of John A. Macdonald. Fleming was also highly motivated to solve the railway scheduling problem, as he had once been stranded at a train station for 16 hours. Oh yes, and he was also a VIP with the CPR.

DIVIDE AND CONQUER. Fleming came up with a plan to divide the world into 24 equal zones. This idea of course corresponded quite nicely with the 24 hours in a day. The man was understandably excited about his revelation and its potential usefulness.

He announced his plan at a meeting of the Canadian Institute for the Advancement of Scientific Knowledge (how's that for an unwieldy name?) in 1879.

BE GONE FROM HERE, YOU HERETIC! Fleming was personally condemned by his fellow scientists and told that his idea was—Gasp!—"contrary to the will of God." Despite that initial reception, standard time, as Fleming's proposal came to be called, was adopted in Canada in 1883. Most other countries in the world followed. And ever since then, trains have run on time—well sometimes.

A SNAPPY KINDA DRESSER. Even though Fleming was an extraordinarily capable man, his wife chose his clothes for him. She probably didn't think she had much choice in the matter. When they were engaged, he paid her a call over the Easter weekend—wearing a pink suit! She must've liked his ZZ Top-style beard, though, because he kept that.

THE LITTLE GIRL WHO NEVER REALLY WAS

Strange but true—one of Canada's most famous people never actually existed.

AN IMAGINARY FRIEND. The most famous person ever to come out of the Canadian Maritimes was Anne Shirley, a little girl who never existed in the first place. Despite this impediment, Anne (of Green Gables, in case you hadn't guessed) was the catalyst for an entire industry that helps to support Prince Edward Island.

MONEY, MONEY, MONEY. The sad irony, though, is that the world's love for Anne and the area where she "lived" has tarnished the Cavendish area in which author Lucy Maud Montgomery created and set Anne of Green Gables. Tens of thousands of tourists—and, of course, tourist dollars—flood the tiny province every summer. An industry has sprung up to meet (a cynic might say "exploit") the tourists' demands.

HUMBLE BEGINNINGS. Anne's origins were humble. She came from a spinster school-teacher's pen. L.M. Montgomery wrote the original *Anne of Green Gables* book in 1905. Two years and many rejection slips later, Montgomery found a publisher willing to take a chance on her story about an optimistic little orphan girl with a love of nature.

DECISION TIME. The publisher—an American firm—offered Montgomery a choice—a flat payment of $500 or royalties of less than a dime on each book sold. She took the royalties and eventually became a very wealthy woman.

POETIC JUSTICE. Anne, of course, is Canadiana personified— just as Huckleberry Finn is Americana. It's a bit ironic then, isn't it, that Montgomery could only find an American publisher while Mark Twain could only find a Canadian publisher.

AND NOW A LITTLE, OR A LOT(!) MORE OF WHAT YOU CAME HERE FOR. The town of Cavendish, Prince Edward Island, has capitalized on Anne's popularity in order to make lots of money. You can find an Anne of Green Gables motel, miniature golf course, candy shops, dozens of souvenir stands, even gas stations and much, much more—way too much more!

ANNE GOES TO PIECES. A first edition of that old Canadian classic *Anne of Green Gables* was recently auctioned off for $24,000 US. The 1908 book is extremely rare because, according to a book dealer, "It's like any good book. When it first came out, it got read to pieces. So there aren't many left."

ANNE LEAVES THE COUNTRY. When the catalogue for the auction came out, announcing that the copy of L.M. Montgomery's beloved story would be for sale, there was a *big* boo-boo in the write-up. *Anne of Green Gables* was mistakenly listed as being "an *American* children's book."

A VICEREGAL READ. Of course, they corrected the grievous error immediately. And it's a good thing, too, or they might have had all of Prince Edward Island Tourism after them. Why, even former Governor General Adrienne Clarkson names *Anne of Green Gables* as one of her favourite reads.

UNDERSTATED IS GOOD TOO. Not all Canadian literary connections are over-the-top. For instance, did you know that the full title of Jules Verne's most famous book (and Walt Disney's even more famous movie) is *Twenty Thousand Leagues under the Sea, or The Marvellous and Exciting Adventures of Pierre Aronnax, Conseil, his Servant, and Ned Land, a Canadian Harpooner?* Doesn't exactly roll off the tongue, but that is the actual title!

DEATH AND DESTRUCTION

No one's going to get out of this life alive, of course,
but Canadian history is peppered with
some outrageous heart-stoppers!

DEATH, AND OTHER LIVELY TOPICS

QUICK AND LOTS OF DEAD. If death and destruction are goals of war, then the Battle of the Plains of Abraham must hold a record for efficiency. More than 1300 men were killed or injured in a fight that was all over in 15 minutes. That's an average of nearly 90 casualties per minute!

UNITED IN DEATH. There were so many corpses that all the remains, French and English together, were buried in a common grave—except for the French leader, Marquis Louis-Joseph de Montcalm. His body was placed in a hole blown into the ground by an English cannonball.

BURIED AND REBURIED. On October 13, General Sir Isaac Brock died while fighting in the War of 1812's Battle of Queenston Heights. Over the next 40 years his body was buried, disinterred and reburied four times!

AND THE *NEXT* YEAR. Almost exactly a year after Brock was killed, Tecumseh, a Native leader and great friend to Canadians, had a premonition of his own death. He died in battle the very next day. That we know for sure. Whatever happened to his body, though, has always been a mystery.

ENOUGH SAID. In early June 1891, a three-word headline in Canadian newspapers said it all. "HE IS DYING." No one needed to be told that it was Sir John A. Macdonald who was about to breathe his last. A few days later, the country's first prime minister lay in state while thousands of mourners paid their respects to the beloved old drunk who had been Canada's leader for nearly 20 years.

STORMY WEATHER. As Macdonald's coffin was being moved to a church for his funeral service, a menacing-looking black cloud formed in the sky over the Parliament Buildings. Minutes later the funeral procession was soaked by torrents of rain from a severe, unexpected and very localized storm. Some said it was as though the heavens had suddenly opened up.

COINCIDENCE? Such a storm is a rarity, but another one occurred on July 22, 1950, near Kingsmere, Québec, at exactly the moment of William Lyon Mackenzie King's death in his home on the shores of Kingsmere Lake. He had been prime minister of Canada for more than 22 years.

DYING WHILE DINING. Sir John Thompson was prime minister of Canada for only two years, from 1892 to 1894. His term was cut short when he died at Windsor Castle in England while dining with the Queen!

THAT'S DEADLY. In 1845, the Church of St. John at New Germany, Nova Scotia, had a little something extra to offer its thirsty parishioners. Bootleggers built fake gravestones in the churchyard cemetery. These bogus markers were hollow and held bottles of hootch. After-service sales were not only convenient, but also discreet.

WEATHER—OR NOT

Pretty much any time, anywhere in Canada, you can talk about the weather and have an interesting conversation. Our weather has often been more than a backdrop to our lives. It has sometimes been an important part of our history.

RAIN, RAIN, IT'LL SOON GO AWAY. By 1932, the terrible effects of the Great Depression had hit the Canadian prairies. The dreadful drought, however, was still in the not-too-distant future. As a matter of fact, on April 22, 1932, it was pouring rain in and around the town of Elgin, Manitoba.

THAT COOKED ALL MY GEESE. After a while, that rainstorm became a thunderstorm. Lightning slashed through the dark skies. One bolt hit and killed a flock of 52 geese. That evening, 52 Elgin families enjoyed a hearty goose dinner.

KILLER HEAT. In 1936, the Great Depression was wreaking havoc on the lives of average Canadians. Then Mother Nature added a one-two punch—no rain and, in early July, a record-setting heat wave.

HOW BAD WAS IT? For days, most of the country cooked in 111°F (44°C) temperatures. By the time things finally cooled off a bit, 780 people had died from the effects of the heat.

NO ORDINARY STORM. Hurricane Hazel hit Canada's largest city, Toronto, on Friday, October 15, 1954. Torrential rains and terrible winds lashed parts of the city. First cars, and then entire homes, were washed away as rivers flooded their banks.

ANY ROOF IN A STORM. People were injured and killed. The storm was so severe in some communities that the "lucky" people were the ones who were able to climb up on the roofs of their houses. There they waited until help arrived.

HURRICANE HEROES. And arrive it did. Many otherwise ordinary Canadians suddenly turned into extraordinary heroes. Jim Crawford was a rookie cop. Herb Jones owned a motorboat. The two men had never met. That night, though, they teamed up and rescued at least 50 stranded souls from certain death.

KEEP ON KEEPING ON. Together Crawford and Jones manoeuvred Jones' small boat through the streets that the hurricane had turned into rivers. On trip after trip, motoring in and out of the worst-hit community, the pair picked terrified people off the roofs of houses where entire families had huddled together so as not to be swept away by the torrents.

WHAT A NIGHT SHIFT. Jim and Herb stayed at it till dawn. Their lives were in peril every minute they were out. By morning the worst of the storm had died down. The two men shook hands and parted—almost forever.

ONE BRIEF REUNION. Twenty-two years later, Jim read in the newspaper that Herb was dying. Jim paid his lifesaving partner one final visit. If it hadn't been for Hurricane Hazel, the two men would probably never have met. As it was, together they saved the future for dozens of Canadian families.

AND MANY, MANY MORE. Herb Jones and Jim Crawford were only two of many people who suddenly became lifesaving heroes on the night of October 15, 1954.

CLASSIC CANADIAN COMBO. Put winter weather and hockey together and what do you get? Well, you get pretty standard Canadian fare, eh? Unless the weather is so severe that it prevents an NHL game from being played. Then it's a history-making legal matter.

WHO YA GONNA CALL? In 1980, the Minnesota North Stars took the Québec Nordiques to court for missing a game. Facing a $64,000 lawsuit, the Québec team hired a weatherman who testified that on the day of the game, the fog in Québec had been so thick that the Nordiques' plane hadn't been able to take off. The judge, no doubt a born-and-bred Canadian and maybe even a hockey fan, readily accepted the weather defence.

NEW YEAR'S WISHES FROM THE WEATHER. Normally a freezing rainstorm would not make headlines in eastern Canada, but from January 5 to 10, 1998, such a storm not only made headlines but also made history.

COLD AND CRUEL. David Phillips, Canada's go-to weather guy, called the storm that dumped 100 millimetres of freezing rain on central and eastern Canada "unprecedented" and "the most spectacular weather event of the century."

CALL IN THE ARMY. Some 15,000 members of Canada's armed forces helped regular community workers cope and clean up. At least 25 people died as a direct result of the weather. Roughly 2 million people were without power—some for more than three weeks.

SMALL MERCIES. Hospitals operated on emergency generators. In some cases their function was reduced to not much more than safe houses for those requiring shelter. On a positive note, the number of car accidents was way down—only because no one could drive on the skating-rink–like conditions.

ICE STORM HEROES. By the time the ice had melted, public opinion was pretty much unanimous—the health care workers had been the heroes of the storm. "Our strength was in our people," an executive at the Montréal General reported.

DEATH IN OTTAWA

It was the first assassination in Canada's history and we're still emotionally involved with it!

A DARK AND CHILLY NIGHT. A very unlikely piece of Canadian history involves Thomas D'arcy McGee, one of the Fathers of Confederation. On the evening of April 7, 1868, McGee was assassinated as he returned home from giving a speech in the House of Commons.

WHO DUNNIT? An Irish immigrant named James Patrick Whelan was arrested, charged with and convicted of the political assassination. Whelan went to the gallows protesting his innocence. Worse, some historians agree. Perhaps that's why Whelan's was the last-ever public execution in Canada.

WHERE'D IT GO? The alleged murder weapon, a Smith & Wesson .32 went missing, from a public perspective anyway, for decades. On May 22, 2005, the gun was put up for auction.

GOING, GOING, GONE...ACROSS TOWN! The auction firm received calls from people in the United States who were interested in taking this piece of gruesome Canadian history out of the country. Ottawa's Bytown Museum made a bold move by publicly soliciting funds to buy the weapon. In the end, the federal Museum of Civilization won the bidding war and bought the gun for $105,000. At least it stayed in Canada.

HAUNTED HERITAGE. The jail where James Patrick Whelan was taken when he was arrested is now a hostel. At one time the place offered free accommodation to anyone who could stay a night in Whelan's cell. No one ever did. If the disembodied voice repeating the Lord's Prayer didn't drive them out, the apparition of Whelan, sitting on the edge of the bed, always did.

CANADIAN CURSES

NO ONE'S GOING TO SWEAR TO THESE BUT…At this writing, the Angus L. Macdonald Bridge has stood for 50 years, despite the fact that it's said to be cursed.

I WOULDN'T DO THAT IF I WERE YOU. From the earliest days, European newcomers to the Nova Scotia area thought life would be much simpler if a bridge connected Halifax to Dartmouth. But a Mi'kmaq chief warned the settlers that this wasn't wise. He declared that trying to span the harbour would lead to three failures. He even went so far as to itemize what they would be. The first would take place during a great wind. The second would happen during a great quiet. The final catastrophe would cause great death.

AND? SO FAR THE CHIEF'S BEEN CORRECT. The winds of a hurricane in 1887 collapsed a railway bridge that had been built across the harbour.

AND THEN…? The temporary bridge that replaced that railway bridge collapsed on an absolutely calm and quiet night.

AND SO? For fifty years people have been successfully crossing from Halifax to Dartmouth and back on the Angus L. Macdonald Bridge. No "great death" so far but…

MEANWHILE, ON THE OTHER SIDE OF THE COUNTRY. Oh, Mr. Fernie, what a lot of trouble you caused by being greedy and not keeping your word! It seems that in the late 1890s, William Fernie promised to marry a Native chief's daughter. He didn't really want a wife; he just wanted the chief to tell him where to dig for coal.

HERE COMES THE BRIDE; THERE GOES THE GROOM. Mere minutes after he learned where the coal was, Fernie was gone—leaving his bride in the lurch with a very angry and vengeful father. The chief decided he would fix that no-good prospector Fernie, and as quick as you could say a bunch of swear words, he placed a curse on the town named after the cad.

HOW BAD WAS THE CURSE? Well, there's probably no such thing as a good curse, but this particular one included the promise of fire, flood and famine. Oh great.

HERE WE GO. For seven years after the chief placed the curse, things went along swimmingly. Then, in 1904, a fire burned the town to the ground. By 1908, residents had rebuilt their community—just in time to be burned down again. In 1916 the Elk River overflowed its banks and flooded most of Fernie.

BUT FAMINE? Then, of course, along came the Dirty Thirties, when many Canadians, including the residents of Fernie, were short of food.

LET'S STOP CURSING. It took the townsfolk another 30-some years after that, but finally they got together with Chief Red Eagle of the Kootenai. He and the mayor of Fernie enjoyed a pipe together, a peace pipe that is. Then they agreed that everyone would play nicely together from then on. That ceremony lifted the curse once and for all!

A PAIN IN THE NECK

SYMPATHY PAINS. Louis Riel was hanged for treason on November 16, 1885, in Regina. As he approached the gallows, the Métis leader carried a statue with him. It was a small likeness of St. Joseph, the patron saint of the Métis. When Riel's neck snapped, the statue dropped from his hands. When it hit the ground, its neck also broke.

BROKEN KEEPSAKE. The head was never found, but the headless St. Joseph was slipped into the coffin and shipped to Riel's family in Fort Garry. Today that broken statue is kept at the St. Boniface Museum, and a replica is on display at Riel House.

MAGIC ROPE. Riel's execution created another interesting "treasure." An enterprising man in the crowd did a hot business selling off pieces the Métis leader's noose. When the salesman reached the end of his rope, so to speak, he just bought more. By the time interest "died down," shall we say, he'd peddled nearly a tonne of hemp souvenirs!

A TOTALLY TASTELESS KEEPSAKE. That ambitious and unscrupulous cad of a rope salesman may have picked up the idea from an 1859 hanging in Brighton, Ontario. After Dr. William King was hanged for murdering his wife, the dead woman's relatives cut up the hangman's rope. They each kept a piece as a souvenir.

DEADMAN'S ISLAND

WHAT'S IN A NAME? Halifax's Deadman's Island isn't really an island. It's a peninsula. Despite this, the place is well named because the land was used as a cemetery for nearly 200 American prisoners of war captured during the War of 1812.

TALK ABOUT DAMAGING PROPERTY VALUES! The burial place was largely ignored until a real estate developer decided Deadman's Island would be an ideal spot for condominiums. Haligonians (as those living in Halifax like to be called) swung into action. After hours of research, a dedicated group proved that Deadman's could not be developed because it already was serving a purpose—it was a cemetery.

LITTLE ALCATRAZ. Over the course of the war, the jail on nearby Melville Island (which really *is* an island) had held more than 8100 American prisoners. Guards used a clever bit of psychology to make sure none of them escaped. They told them that the waters around the island were full of sharks! That would make prison seem like an inviting option.

IN YOU GO. By the time the war was over, many of the American soldiers had died. Their bodies were taken to Deadman's Island and unceremoniously dumped into unmarked graves.

RIP, 193 YEARS LATER. On American Memorial Day in 2005, the Year of the Veteran, the last of the bitterness from the War of 1812 was finally laid to rest. A group of politicians, military and other VIPs from both Canada and the United States gathered to honour the men buried there and to unveil a plaque commemorating their lives and their deaths.

OUR SENSE OF HISTORY WON. Take *that* you nasty would-be condominium builder!!

APPEASING THE GOD OF PROGRESS

THERE SHE BLOWS! July 1, 1958, was celebrated as Dominion Day in most of Canada. But in Cornwall, Ontario, something much more important was happening. By early morning 25,000 people had gathered on a dike. At 8:00 AM there was an ear-splitting blast. The crowd cheered and clapped and hugged each other in celebration. They'd waited for years to hear that explosion. It was Inundation Day.

LET'S GET GOING! The St. Lawrence River was on its way to becoming the St. Lawrence Seaway. Construction of the Seaway had begun in earnest four years earlier. What a great thing it was going to be. Electricity would be cheaper, shipping would be easier. This was post-war Canada, and progress-at-any-cost was the ultimate goal. The people of Cornwall not only accepted that fact, but embraced it.

GOING. But not everyone in the area was happy. Some were heartbroken. And it's no wonder. The towns and villages that 6500 people had called home, some for a lifetime, were about to be flooded. On purpose. That burst of dynamite had blown apart a dam.

GONE. Within hours, 9000 hectares of Canadian soil and a dozen communities, or at least parts of them, were under water; 525 houses had been hauled away and 394 new ones built; 60 kilometres of Highway 2, one of the oldest roads in Ontario, had been torn up, as well as 70 kilometres of railway track.

DIG THIS. The Lachine Rapids, two kilometres of roiling rapids, had been silenced, and a 250-square-metre lake, St. Lawrence Lake, had been created. An entire cemetery had been dug up and moved. Other graves now lay under 20 metres of water at the bottom of the deep new lake.

IN THE NAME OF PROGRESS. Schools and churches had been demolished. New ones would be built in New Town #1 and New Town #2, where the residents would be relocated. Once-thriving communities were gone—forever. No wonder so many people were so sad.

PART OF CANADA'S HERITAGE. But all of that seemed to be forgotten on June 26, 1959. A proud Prime Minister John Diefenbaker, along with President Dwight Eisenhower of the United States and Queen Elizabeth II, officially opened the St. Lawrence Seaway. The Canadian economy has been heavily dependent on the seaway for nearly half a century now.

DIVING HEAVEN? Today the drowned towns are pretty much forgotten. Of course, the folks who lived in those lost communities, or whose relatives once did, still remember the places. But there's another group who can't forget those villages or the people who once called them home. You see, St. Lawrence Lake has become a popular spot for scuba divers.

OR DIVING HELL? They love to swim about the flooded relics— except when they're spooked by strange sensations they sometimes get down there. But maybe they only *feel* that they're being watched. Maybe they've been listening to too many sailors' stories about seeing strange lights deep below the lake's surface and hearing voices coming from beneath the waves.

MEN, WOMEN
AND MONSTERS

*Of course, our land has been here a lot longer than we
human beings have been on it, so the story the land has
to tell is even longer—and stranger!*

LONG, LONG AGO

REALLY OLD NEWS. Attention to those dwelling in the prairie provinces. It's a good thing that you're not a lot older, because 35 million years ago, ferocious giant pigs roamed the Canadian prairies.

DUMB AND DUMBER (OR TWEEDLE DUM AND TWEEDLE DUMBER). The stegosaurus was the dumbest being ever to roam Canada. The prehistoric brute weighed in at 5.9 tons but had a 70 gram brain. (Could he even have figured out where to scratch if he itched?)

GIGANTIC HERITAGE. The beaver, Canada's national symbol, is smarter than that, but it too is descended from giants that once roamed the earth.

BEAVERS MADE US WHAT WE ARE TODAY. Without beavers and the fur traders who killed them, there might not even be a Canada as we know it. By 1900 the industrious creatures were almost extinct. They managed to hang on till the 1930s, when the work of Grey Owl, that great Canadian fake (see "Lies that Would (or Should) Not Die"), managed to revive their numbers.

OOPS! In 1946, South American officials decided that a fur-trade industry was exactly what their economy needed. They took 25 pair of beavers from Canada. Those original animals settled right into their new home. Soon they multiplied and multiplied and multiplied! With no natural enemies in Chile or Argentina, the buck-toothed rodents are now considered a plague and are even a serious threat to the rain forests.

WHERE THE BUFFALO ROAM. Very few mammals managed to survive the Ice Age, but the buffalo certainly did. They adapted so well that explorer Alexander Henry wrote of seeing buffalo herds so enormous they covered the ground for "as far as the eye could see."

LET'S EXPLORE!

As anyone who's been through the Canadian school system knows, our explorers are a proud part of our heritage. But some of those explorers, we're just starting to hear about.

GET SERIOUS. For several years now, amateur historian Gavin Menzies has been pestering professional historians with a crazy theory about Zheng He, a Chinese explorer who Menzies says landed somewhere on Canada's East Coast—in 1421!

IN 1492, COLUMBUS SAILED THE OCEAN BLUE. If Menzies is correct, then Zheng He clearly beat Columbus to North America—by a good 70 years.

SHOW ME THE PROOF. On May 16, 2005, the historians who've been bothered by Menzies and his pesky theory were startled by the announcement that he had found the remains of a naval base, which Menzies claimed the Chinese explorer had built while he was in Canada. The serious ones were fascinated, and as of this writing a team of archeologists is preparing to head for the site. So, you see, history can still be news.

ON THE OTHER COAST. Chinese explorers may also have visited Canada's West Coast—in the year 449. Sound too fantastic to be true? Maybe so, but the claim seems to be backed up by the writings of a Buddhist monk named Hoei Shin, who wrote detailed accounts of his voyages. And those reports weren't published in some tabloid newspaper. They're stored in Beijing's national library.

WHAT'S IN A NAME? On November 17, 1685, the settlement of Trois-Rivières was a happy place. Marie and Rene La Vérendrye became proud parents—again. This was lucky number 13.

You'd think that they might have called it quits, but instead they named their baby boy Pierre.

RAISE 'EM RIGHT. Now Rene and Marie were clearly not the sort to mollycoddle their children, and by the time Pierre was 14, he had finished his education and was in the army. However, Pierre soon found that his career kept him away from home more than he'd have liked (military service will do that). By 1712 he had left the army, married and settled down to farm a small plot of land near Trois-Rivières.

YOU CAN TAKE THE MAN OFF THE FARM, BUT... It would seem that Pierre enjoyed domestic life—for a while, anyway. He and his wife soon had six children. But when Pierre turned 40, he had a bit of a mid-life crisis. As buying a red convertible wasn't an option, the farmer headed out to try his hand in the wilds. In doing so, he became the first Canadian-born explorer.

NOPE, THAT WON'T DO EITHER. For a time, Pierre teamed up with one of his brothers at a trading post in Thunder Bay, but even that didn't satisfy him. Next he went back to New France and talked to the governor about financing for a trip to explore farther west. Pierre must have dropped in at home after that, because when he left again he took two of his sons with him.

WHERE ARE THEY? Together the La Vérendrye father-and-sons team searched for a route to the Pacific Ocean and for a tribe of Natives they had been told about—the Mandans. These people were reported to be blue-eyed, light-skinned, blonde-haired. Surely such fair folks would know of a route across Canada.

KEEP ON LOOKING. Pierre and his sons travelled for more than a decade but never did find what they were looking for. By the time they were through, though, they had travelled farther west than any non-Native ever had.

THERE GOES THE MARRIAGE. Poor Marie, Pierre's wife, had died in the meantime, and Pierre was now well into his 50s. He must have felt that it was time to give up the life of an explorer and settle down again because that's exactly what he did—for a while. Why, he even remarried.

ONE LAST JAUNT. But then the old restlessness hit once more, and Pierre wanted to get out into the wilds again. As a matter of fact, he was planning his next venture on December 5, 1749, when he died.

LOOK AT THAT! Pierre's story might have ended there except that on February 16, 1913, some children playing in South Dakota came across a lead tablet on a hillside. The letters etched into the tablet proclaimed that on March 30, 1743, the La Vérendryes had claimed that land for France.

FOREVER MARKED. A South Dakota service club erected a marker on the site proclaiming that the tablet had been "the first written record of the visit of white men to South Dakota." After all his efforts and frustrations, it's a safe bet that Pierre La Vérendrye would be tickled to know at least one of his accomplishments has been so permanently recognized.

BORN TOO LATE. Pierre La Vérendrye and Samuel Hearne never knew one another. Hearne was just a lad when La Vérendrye died. It's too bad things worked out that way because they likely would have enjoyed one another's company. Like La Vérendrye, Hearne joined the military as a youngster. But after that, rather than exploring independently as La Vérendrye had done, Hearne joined the Hudson's Bay Company.

JOIN THE COMPANY. Hearne was a young man who showed great promise, so the HBC factor chose him to lead an expedition in search of the great mineral riches they wanted so badly to find.

Hearne headed out on the first journey in 1769, but the Native man the factor had chosen as a guide soon abandoned the poor explorer.

TRY AGAIN. Hearne obviously found his way back to the HBC post because the next year the factor chose another guide, and away they went a second time. This time Hearne was robbed before he was abandoned. Not surprisingly, the would-be explorer told the factor he'd choose his own Native guide for the next attempt.

MAYBE SOME INDEPENDENCE IS A GOOD THING. The guide Hearne chose was sure he had the answer to a successful expedition—take women, lots of women. After all, the women carried loads, pitched tents and mended clothing. What more could a company of explorers need? Apparently not much because Hearne was the first non-Native to see the Arctic Ocean. Of course, Hearne claimed the ocean for England.

IT GETS BETTER. By the time the men and women arrived back home at Fort Prince of Wales on Hudson's Bay, they had been away for a year and a half and had walked 5600 kilometres. Oh, and the women must have done more than just carry, pitch tents and mend because there were several children to look after on the trip home!

MARITAL BLISS, EARLY CANADIAN STYLE

A LITTLE LOCAL GOSSIP. In 1610, explorer Samuel de Champlain went home to France for a visit. While he was there, he took a wife—the lovely Helene by name. It was kind of an odd coupling, even for that era. You see, although Samuel was about 40 years old then, Helene was a child of 12!

GOLD DIGGER? Some say that Champlain was only after Helene's dowry. Hmmmm, maybe so. His money for explorations *was* running a bit low at the time.

WELL, THEY TRIED. In 1620, 10 years after they had married, Helene boarded a boat and made her way to New France to be at Samuel's side. She didn't like it there very much, though, and just four years later she left New France and went back to "old" France.

SOMETHING IN THE WATER? In 1799, David Thompson, another explorer, also took a wife. Thompson managed to control the joy he felt on his wedding day—at least when he noted the happy occasion in his diary. His journal entry states: "On this day married Charlotte Small." Charlotte was 13 years old!

BUT THIS ONE WAS REAL. Unlike Mr. and Mrs. de Champlain, the Thompsons' marriage was an actual relationship, not simply a business arrangement. Although David did father a few little ones out of wedlock, he and Charlotte stayed together until death parted them...three months apart. They had 13 children.

SOMETHING'S AFOOT

Mythical beasts have roamed the world since the beginning of time. Canada, never a country to be left out of anything, boasts a number of the big brutes. Cadboro Bay on Vancouver Island is home to a water monster named Cadborosaurus or Caddy, and Kempenfelt Kelly is the darling of Lake Simcoe. But arguably the coolest legendary monster doesn't live in the water.

A BIG, SHY FELLOW. Sasquatch, Wild Man, the Abominable Snowman, Bigfoot…all words to describe the same beast. In Canada he's called Sasquatch, a Salish word meaning "wild man." Native folklore is full of references to the big, hairy and *very* elusive beast.

EARLY SIGHTING. Explorer David Thompson (1770–1857) was friendly with the Natives, and, as good friends should, they warned him about a giant, apelike monster that lived in the mountain forests. Their stories about Sasquatch made it clear that they totally believed in the beast's existence. And that they were totally terrified of the thing.

DOUBTING THOMPSON. Thompson, a logical man, clearly questioned the reality of the Native stories and noted in his journal, "This is no doubt some Animal of their…Fables." On January 7, 1811, however, Thompson lost his scepticism and became the first non-Native to record evidence of the gigantic beast's existence.

AND THIS IS WHAT HE WROTE. "I saw the Track of a large Animal—has 4 large Toes, 3 or 4 In [inches] long & a small Nail at the end of each; the Ball of his Foot sank abt 3 In deeper than his Toes; the hinder part of his Foot did not mark well. The whole is abt 14 In long by 8 In wide & very much resembles a large Bear's Track…"

CANADA'S NESSIE. The big hairy guy certainly isn't the only monster in British Columbia. Early settlers were also warned about a giant serpent-like creature living at the bottom of Lake Okanagan. Natives explained that this "snake in the lake" had been there for hundreds of years.

NO JOKE. Those settlers (and their descendents) took these warnings seriously because they named the beast Ogopogo and made a law to protect it from capture or even harassment.

JUST HOW MANY ARE THERE? Over the years, water monsters have been reported in a number of Canadian lakes. Ontario seems to have more than its fair share of the beasts, but the big brutes have also been spotted in Manitoba and the Maritimes. Let's hope these monsters never decide to get together for a family reunion.

Some of the critters sharing our country are all too real.

A SMALLER NEMESIS. Only two topics are guaranteed to unite all Canadians—a disdain for Toronto and a loathing of mosquitoes. Of the two issues, our hatred for the pesky critters apparently goes back further. In the early 1800s, around the time he met the Sasquatch, explorer David Thompson reported, "The air is thick" with mosquitoes and "there is no cessation…from them. Smoke is no relief, they can stand more smoke than we can…"

BUG OFF! With a problem this bad and this longstanding, it shouldn't be much of a surprise that a Canadian invented the most effective mosquito repellent in the world—Muskol. Perhaps it's only surprising that the solution didn't come for another 150 itchy, bug-filled summers!

MADELEINE'S A HEROINE

Joan of Arc, eat your heart out!
We have Madeleine de Vercheres on our side.

HOME ALONE. Madeleine Jarret Tarieu was just 14 years old in October 1692 when she was left in charge at home. Madeleine's father was away at work, i.e., he was serving in the military. On the day of Madeleine's most excellent adventure, you could say that her mother had gone shopping, except that "shopping" in this case meant travelling upriver to Montréal for winter supplies.

DETAILS, DETAILS. And "the home" Madeleine was left responsible for was Fort Vercheres.

SO THE STORY GOES. Madeleine's adventure that day has become a Canadian legend, and there are many different versions of it by now. All agree, though, that the girl was outside the walls of the fort when the Iroquois suddenly attacked.

IT'S CERTAINLY DRAMATIC ANYWAY. One particularly detailed retelling of the tale has the girl wearing a scarf around her neck that day. At the sound of the first bullet, Madeleine ran for the fort's gate, her scarf flying out behind her.

NARROW ESCAPE. She was within reach of the gate when an Iroquois warrior grabbed at her neckerchief. Madeleine ripped off the scarf and managed to free herself from the enemy's grasp. As soon as she was inside the fort, she fired the canon. She hoped that the blast would scare the Iroquois and attract help.

VIRTUALLY SINGLE-HANDED. Madeleine armed her younger brother, an elderly man and a couple of soldiers who were staying in the fort. The motley group must have fired enough rounds to convince the enemy that the place was much better fortified than it actually was, because the attackers soon retreated. A courageous and quick-thinking teenaged girl had successfully fought off the enemy and saved the settlement.

AND THEN...? When Madeleine's father died, the government of France transferred his pension to her as thanks for having saved the fort that day. Madeleine remained single for many years, but legend has it that when she did eventually marry, she once had to beat off a man who was attacking her husband.

WHAT A ROLE MODEL. Throughout World War II, the Canadian government used posters featuring Madeleine's image, including the scarf that had almost caused her demise, to recruit women for the war effort.

MAKING HISTORY

Even before Canada became a country,
and in the nearly 140 years since Confederation,
there have been people here who made such a difference that
they've actually made history. Unfortunately, not all of the
differences those folks made were good. Some were.
Others weren't. Read on and pick through a few of each.

GOTTA LOVE THE EGO. Without the Hudson's Bay Company, Canadian history books just wouldn't be the same. And without Sir George Simpson as governor-in-chief of the HBC for nearly 40 years, the company wouldn't have been nearly as important to Canadian history—or nearly as colourful. Sir George insisted that a pair of Highland pipers go with him as he toured about the Canadian wilderness—even when he was travelling by canoe!

LIKE FATHER, LIKE SON. George Simpson married his cousin and fathered five children. He was also the father of at least five illegitimate children, which is especially meaningful when you realize that George himself was also illegitimate.

A PIONEER OF A DIFFERENT SORT. Grace Lockhart made history when she graduated from Mount Allison University in Sackville, New Brunswick, in 1874. Lockhart became the first woman in Canada to earn a university degree. Young women today would find it difficult to follow exactly in Miss Lockhart's footsteps, though, as the degree she was awarded was an MLA or Mistress of Liberal Arts. Thankfully such a sexist title no longer exists.

A CROOK BY ANY OTHER NAME. Lucien Rivard was a "thug"— at least that's how he was described in the press during the early 1960s. By March 1965, he'd been caught running drugs— *again*—and was cooling his heels in Montréal's Bourdeaux jail.

The guards must've thought he was a jock, too. On the evening of March 2, 1965, they gave him permission to flood the prison's skating rink.

HE'S OUTA THERE. But Rivard apparently wanted to run, not skate. He used the garden hose the guards had given him for the rink to scale the wall instead. Within minutes he'd broken out of jail. Perhaps the guards weren't surprised. It would've been tough to make ice that night as the temperature was well above freezing.

AN UNLIKELY AND UNFORGETTABLE HERO. Eighteen-year-old boys are such a crazy bunch, aren't they? Imagine anyone thinking that he could run all the way across Canada! That would be a feat even for a healthy person, but 18-year-old Terry Fox, a one-legged cancer survivor, decided he had to try.

MUST'VE RAISED HIM RIGHT. Terry was determined to raise Canadians' awareness of the deadly disease that had caused so much suffering and had cost him his leg when he was 18. He also wanted to raise money—lots of money—for cancer research so that the terrible disease could be stopped.

HE REALLY STARTED SOMETHING. On April 12, 1980, Terry Fox started his Marathon of Hope by dipping his artificial leg into the Atlantic Ocean. He ran along Canadian highways for the equivalent of a marathon a day—every day. No one who saw him run could ever forget the sight. That awkward, hop-step, painful-looking gait etched itself into the minds—and hearts—and wallets—of Canadians.

GO, BOY! Day by day, town by town, city by city, Terry's efforts stole our collective hearts. One uncomfortable step at a time, his mission was being accomplished. This young man had succeeded in putting a face to a disease that was still only whispered about. Financial support for cancer research poured in.

FELLED. By September 1, Fox had reached Thunder Bay, Ontario, an amazing 5376 kilometres from St. John's—two-thirds of the way across this huge country of ours. That evening, Canadians watched in horror as television news reports showed images of their newest hero strapped to a stretcher.

DREAMS NEVER DIE, JUST THE DREAMER. The cancer that had taken Terry Fox's leg had returned—to his lungs this time. Terry died on June 28, 1981. He had raised $25 million for cancer research and left an astonishing legacy. Every September, fund-raising runs commemorating his courage and determination are held in most Canadian communities as well as more than 50 other countries, with profits going to cancer research.

WHAT GIGANTIC FOOTSTEPS TO FILL. Terry Fox became an idol to a generation of Canadian young people, especially, of course, other cancer patients. Steve Fonyo, who had also lost a leg to cancer, decided to complete Terry's run. And he made it!

THE JOURNEY FOR LIVES. Steve Fonyo ran through frigid temperatures and good old Canadian spring blizzards. On May 29, 1985, he made headlines around the world as he finished his run by dipping his artificial leg into the Pacific Ocean. Fonyo's tribute to Terry Fox was complete. And he had raised $13 million for cancer research.

RUN OUT. After running from the north to the south of Great Britain in 1987, Fonyo declared that his fundraising marathons were over.

MAN IN MOTION. Terry Fox and Rick Hansen met and became friends on the basketball court. Both were determined athletes with more physical challenges than most other competitors. While Steve Fonyo was completing his run, Rick Hansen set out to go around the world—in his wheelchair. His journey lasted more than two years. He travelled through 34 countries and raised $20 million dollars to support spinal cord injury research.

DID YOU  KNOW?

MAN ON A MISSION. It was the dead of winter, 1908, when Wilbur Wolfendon's bride arrived in Winnipeg from her homeland of Holland. Wilbur was there to greet the lovely lass. He'd *walked* to the 'Peg from Calgary—more than 1330 kilometres!

LONG-AGO-PERSON-FOUND

LAST SUPPER. Kwaday Dan Ts'inchi was in his late teens or early 20s that summer. The young man was exploring the Tatshenshini-Alsek Park in northwestern British Columbia. He stopped for a meal—asparagus and fresh glacial water. It wasn't much, but he didn't need anything more. He'd been eating well throughout the trip. There'd been one meal of deer meat, another of salmon and lots of luscious berries.

WHAT A FIND! After eating, he lay down to rest a while. And that was the last thing the explorer ever did. How do we know this? His perfectly preserved, 500-year-old body was found in August 1999. He was immediately dubbed Kwaday Dan Ts'inchi by the Champagne-Aishihik First Nations, which means "long-ago-person-found."

POKING AROUND. Since then the young man's corpse has been subject to a host of indignities in the name of science. By examining his digestive system, scientists have discovered what season it was when he died and what he last ate. They were puzzled, though, about what might have killed the traveller, especially as he hadn't been injured.

SNOW DAY. Geological Survey of Canada scientists reason that, even though it was summer when Kwaday Dan Ts'inchi died, it was also just at the start of the Little Ice Age. While he was sleeping off his asparagus and water meal, it likely started to snow. He could have died quickly and quietly of hypothermia. The result? One small, unique, perfectly preserved piece of Canadian history.

AN AUTHOR BY ANY OTHER NAME

WHAT'S IN A NAME? Young Billy Falkner came to Canada in 1918. By the time he left again a mere six months later, he had become William Faulkner. And he had written his first bit of fiction.

REJECTED. It seems that Faulkner wanted to become a World War I fighter pilot. He had applied to the American armed forces, but they'd turned him down because he was too small.

TAKE ME! TAKE ME! The future novelist decided to try his luck in Canada. He thought that the Canadian forces wouldn't take an American citizen, so young Billy changed the spelling of his name and adopted a British accent (which must have sounded pretty funny over his southern drawl!). Then William Faulkner headed to the recruiting office in Toronto. A week later he was wearing a uniform.

AND THEN...IT WAS OVER. But Billy Falkner, or William Faulkner as he preferred to be known by then, never wore the one uniform he really wanted—a pilot's uniform. The war ended before he could be trained.

LET'S PRETEND. Despite the huge disappointment, Faulkner made more than the best of his experiences in Canada. He pulled together bits and pieces of a pilot's uniform and had his portrait taken—complete with a cane to imply he'd been injured in action.

DID I TELL YOU ABOUT THE TIME I...? As the years passed, Faulkner's fictions about his service in Canada became more and more inventive. By that time, he had really learned how to spin a yarn! In fact, he won the 1949 Nobel Prize for Literature for his body of work.

ODD DUCKS WE HAVE CALLED OUR OWN

The following is a list of some really strange characters in Canada's history. They're listed in alphabetical order because there was no other way to decide who should be Number One!

WILLIAM ABERHART (1878–1943). Good old Bible Bill was well ahead of his time. During the Depression he gave out "free money." Today, radio station contests copy his idea.

JEFFREY AMHERST (1717–97). This British general, who was promoted to commander-in-chief in 1758 after he successfully captured the French town of Louisbourg, on Cape Breton, assured his sister that vampires lived in Germany.

AMOR DE COSMOS (1825–97). The former Bill Smith was the second in a long line of rather odd British Columbia leaders. As he aged he became vain enough to apply liberal (and obvious!) amounts of black shoe polish to his beard. He refused to ride tram cars because he was terrified of electricity.

HERBERT HOLT (1856–1941). In his early days, some might have called Holt a "businessman's businessman" because in the 1920s he owned nearly everything in Montréal. Eventually, because he had so much power, he became pretty unpopular. How unpopular? Well, at least three people tried to kill him. Still, though, they might've laughed when he declared the cornerstone he placed in the Royal Bank on St. James Street in Montréal was "well and truly laid."

IZAAK WALTON KILLAM (1885–1955). For a while, Killam was the richest man in Canada. He was instrumental in setting up the Canada Council, despite the fact that his love of culture began and ended with potboiler detective stories.

SIR HENRY PELLATT (1859–1939). Only an ego as enormous as Pellat's could've built Casa Loma, "the grotesque, ersatz castle" on a hill in Toronto.

AIMEE SEMPLE MCPHERSON (1890–1944). Here's a "small-town-girl-makes-good-in-LA" story with a twist. Aimee Semple McPherson was a hellfire preacher who established the Angelus Temple of the Four Square Gospel in Los Angeles. She did rather well for herself—at least until those pesky scandals destroyed the credibility she apparently had.

EQUAL OPPORTUNITIES. Lest we give the impression that it's only Canadian *women* who can lead their flock astray, we must mention Brother Andre (1845–1937). He was a faith healer who was exceptionally popular with Québec's working class. His diet consisted mainly of bread that had been soaked in watered-down milk, black coffee and, towards the end of his life, flour in a warm brine solution. It makes you wonder if any of his faith-healing "solutions" were any more reasonable than his diet.

GEORGE WESTON (1864–1924). The man created a business empire that is still impressive today. Weston died of pneumonia after walking for kilometres through a terrible blizzard. He hadn't wanted to spend money on a taxi.

BE A SPORT

*Canadians believe we're known for our hockey,
but there are a couple of other games people
couldn't play if we hadn't invented them.*

HOCKEY

Who invented hockey? The Canadians did, of course!
What? You say it was the Danes???

HOCKEY NIGHT IN DENMARK? Canadians may *not* have invented hockey! A small piece of art in a Copenhagen museum shows two skaters holding sticks and facing each other in apparent anticipation of a puck being dropped. The image was painted in AD 1000!

CALL IN THE ARMY TEAM. The earliest hockey games on this side of the pond were probably played by English soldiers stationed here during the 1800s. The rest, as they say, is history—Canadian history and so, of course, we have to debate it.

WHICH RINK? The Windsor and Halifax-Dartmouth regions of Nova Scotia, Kingston in Ontario, and Montréal all claim that they have proof the first hockey game was played in *their* area. Then, probably just to annoy us hockey-mad Canadians, the National Gallery of Art in Washington, DC, announced that it owns a painting of hockey being played in Virginia during 1835!

HERE COMES STANLEY. We do know that the Stanley Cup was first awarded in 1893—to the best amateur team. In 1910 the cup was taken over by the newly formed National Hockey Association, which evolved into the National Hockey League a few years later. And it was awarded every year after that—except for 1919. The Department of Health cancelled hockey that year. It didn't want crowds gathering anywhere for fear of the flu epidemic spreading to even more people.

SHOW ME THE MONEY. Oh, and of course the Stanley Cup wasn't awarded in 2005 either—thanks to that pesky lockout by the owners!

GO FANS GO. On November 22, 2003, more than 50,000 Canadians made history by forming the largest crowd to attend a hockey game. The fans braved –40° weather to watch an outdoor game between the Montreal Canadiens' and Edmonton Oilers' old-timers, followed by a regular NHL game between the Canadiens and Oilers. (Hometown Oilers won the old-timers match, while the Canadiens won the game that counted for season points.)

DID YOU  KNOW?

WRONG AGAIN. British Columbia's Chief Dan George once pointed out that from the earliest times to the present, European depictions of Natives with bows and arrows have been inaccurate. The Natives hunted with their bows held horizontally, while Europeans held them vertically. The newcomers' egos obviously interfered with their eyesight because paintings consistently show Natives holding the bow in the European fashion.

BASKETS AND BOWLS

*How sporting of us. Okay, so maybe we didn't invent hockey, but
Canadians definitely changed the course of sporting history by
inventing both basketball and five-pin bowling. And we might
even hold bragging rights to America's favourite game—baseball.*

LET'S CELEBRATE! A day off work in the summer is a fine thing.
Too bad we don't still celebrate Militia Muster Day, like they did
on June 4, 1838. The government declared that day a holiday to
celebrate the victorious end of the 1837 Rebellion. In Beachville,
Ontario, the folks gathered on a farmer's pasture.

PLAY BALL! They were there to enjoy a ball game played on
a diamond-shaped field. There were two teams consisting of
a batter, a "thrower," bases (four of them!) a catcher and out-
fielders. That game occurred a year before baseball was
"invented" in the United States.

NECESSITY, THE MOTHER OF INVENTION. In 1891, James
Naismith was faced with what we nowadays like to call a "challenge." Of course, Naismith might have used stronger words to
describe the problem he had getting members of his all-male sec-
retarial class to participate in physical education classes during
the winter.

THE BRUTES. These future secretaries were big, burly, tough
guys. They may have been co-operative at their typewriters, but
when they put their collective foot down about something,
apparently they were not the sort to be trifled with. And they
were adamantly opposed to the calisthenics and drills Naismith
had them do. Who can blame them?

SAFETY FIRST. Naismith worked out the fundamentals of a chal-
lenging game that could be played indoors. Knowing that players

throwing each other down on a hard floor could cause a few problems, Naismith made sure the game was free of tackling. Considering that the men had been a bit of a pain, you have to give Naismith a point or two for thoughtfulness.

TAKE 'EM TO COURT. By the time those macho student secretaries appeared for their next physical education class, James Naismith was ready for them. He had a soccer ball, and two peach baskets were nailed up on the gymnasium wall. The name of the game was to get the ball into the basket—or, sensibly, basketball.

INVENTED FOR MEN. PERFECTED BY WOMEN. People loved Naismith's game. Basketball teams formed all over the world, but by the inventor's own admission, "the finest team ever to set foot on a basketball court" was a women's team—the Edmonton Commercial Graduates. The "Grads" played a total of 522 games. They won an incredible 502 of those games—a record that has never been beaten anywhere, in any sport.

KNOCK 'EM DOWN. By the early 1900s, ten-pin bowling was a popular game. It was even considered quite sophisticated. Why, Tom Ryan's alley in downtown Toronto even offered the bowlers fine musical accompaniment. Ryan hired an orchestra to serenade them. Unfortunately, in order to knock down ten big bowling pins, bowling balls had to be pretty large. The racket they made as they rolled down the alleys drowned out the pretty music.

QUIET IN THE LANES, PLEASE. But that noise was nothing compared to the clatter as the pins fell. Something had to be done, and Mr. Ryan was just the man to do it. He shaved down the bowling balls till they were roughly a quarter of their original size, and he took away half the pins. Voila! A new sport—five-pin bowling—had been invented. Its popularity soared and the rest, as they say, is history.

CANADA'S (OTHER) FAVOURITE PASTIME?

WHAT A BABE! Babe Ruth hit his first-ever professional home run at a baseball field on Toronto Island.

AROUND YOU GO. During the 1950s, O.C.S. Robertson was a captain in the Canadian Navy. Even though he had quite a few initials in his name, he was an excellent sailor and just an all-round nice guy. How do we know this? In 1954, Robertson commanded HMCS *Labrador* as it made history by being the first ship to sail around North America in a single voyage.

SKILLED SAILOR, YES, BUT NICE GUY? In 1960, the American Navy asked Robertson to lead an expedition through the Northwest Passage. During the trip, Robertson treated the men under his command to a game of baseball—at the North Pole.

PLAY BALL. The captain laid out the "field" so that first base was in the world's eastern hemisphere and third base in the western hemisphere. The International Date Line ran down a point between home and first base. That meant that the ball could be hit into tomorrow!

TAKE ME TO
YOUR LEADERS

First, the land that would be Canada had a king—
several kings. When it became a country, it was ruled by a
queen. And then we had prime ministers. But one of them
was a King too. Mackenzie King. Are you confused yet?

THE ROYALS

*Love 'em or hate 'em, the British monarchy
has always been important to Canada.*

THE FIRST ROYAL VISIT. Prince William, not the handsome
young son of today's Prince Charles, but the man who eventually
became King William IV, was the first member of the royal family
to set foot on Canadian soil when he visited parts of Newfoundland and Nova Scotia in 1786. This wasn't a royal visit, though.
The prince was here as part of a naval contingent serving in
North America and the West Indies.

AND THEN...? The royal visit in 1939 was an occasion for much
greater attention to detail. The Montreal Hussars, a mounted
regiment, was part of the welcoming ceremony, but then the
unthinkable happened—one of the horses became restless. Not
willing to take any chances on something untoward happening
in the presence of King George VI and his wife, organizers ban-
ished the excited horse from its place in the parade.

WHAT TO DO, WHAT TO DO? But this left a gaping hole in the
formation. Something had to be done, and quickly! With just
hours to spare, a quieter horse was found, but it was white! The
rest of the Hussars' mounts were dark.

DYEING TO FIX IT. The regiment's commander did the only
thing he could do under the circumstances. He had a local hair-
dresser dye the substitute steed to match the others. The rest of
the royal visit to this colony went off without a hitch!

ROYAL ON THE RANGE. King Edward VIII was still the Prince
of Wales when he bought himself a little spread near Calgary,
which he named the EP Ranch. He didn't keep the throne very

long because Wallis Simpson promised to provide him with a lot more fun in his life. He kept the Alberta ranch till the 1960s, but only visited it five times in total.

ROYAL CANADIAN BIRTH? While the Nazis occupied the Netherlands during World War II, some members of the Dutch royal family escaped to Canada. Princess Juliana and Prince Bernhard of Holland were living in Ottawa during 1943 when a blessed royal event occurred—their daughter, Princess Margriet, was born! To ensure the baby was a Dutch citizen, the Canadian government declared their hospital room to be Dutch territory for the birth.

BLOOMIN' THANKS! Every year since then, Ottawa's annual Tulip Fest reminds us beautifully of Holland's appreciation. As an everlasting "thank you" to the Canadian soldiers who freed their country from the Nazis, and for the kindness that Canada showed the royal family while they were living here, the Dutch sent us 100,000 tulip bulbs. They send an additional 10,000 every year for the Tulip Fest.

DID YOU  KNOW?

IN HIS OTHER LIFE. There's nothing quite like hunkering down with a good thriller on a cold winter's night. And one of the best is a book called *The Thirty-nine Steps*. It was written by John Buchan. Did you know that he was Canada's Governor General from 1935 to 1940. It's not too surprising, then, that it was Buchan who created the Governor General's Literary Awards.

POLITICIANS AND OTHER STRANGE BEDFELLOWS

To put it politely, Canada's prime ministers have been an assortment of rather odd ducks.

HE WAS NUMBER ONE. Sir John A. Macdonald, Canada's first prime minister, is often described as being "all too human." Maybe that's the nicest way to say Sir John loved to drink— frequently and to excess. He also liked to accept bribes.

BUT HE'S STILL THE MAN. Despite his flaws, the people clearly loved their leader. They elected him three times. Of course, Canadians today can't vote for him, but they can buy a Sir John A. Macdonald bobble-head doll—from either the very Canadian CBC or the very American WalMart.

REJECTION ISSUES? Edward Blake became the leader of the Liberal party on May 4, 1880. He's the only person ever to have held that office and not become prime minister.

THAT WAS QUICK. Sir Charles Tupper, a Conservative, holds the record for the shortest time in the prime minister's office— 69 days during 1896.

GOING FOR THE RECORD. Sir Wilfrid Laurier was elected next, and he holds the record for the longest unbroken term in the prime minister's office.

FROM THE MOUTHS OF BABES. Laurier loved kids. While visiting Saskatoon in the summer of 1910, he stopped to talk to a newspaper carrier. The lad told Laurier of his own plan to become prime minister. Laurier declared that "the boy was filled with interesting political ideas." After a time the child excused himself, saying "Well, Mr. Prime Minister, I can't waste any more time on you. I must get back to work."

AND THE PUNCH LINE? The paper boy was John Diefenbaker, who, just as he predicted he would, became prime minister.

A NEW WORD. Diefenbaker was Canada's political leader from June 1957 to April 1963. At the time, the Cold War was heating up. Nervous citizens were building bomb shelters in their basements and backyards, which soon became known as "Diefenbunkers."

A NEW NAME. Lester B. Pearson joined the Air Force during World War I, but it was Mike Pearson who served. Pearson's commanding officer assigned the nickname "Mike" after declaring that he couldn't imagine a pilot named "Lester."

WHAT A SPORT. By any name, Pearson was a jock. Like the good Canadian boy he was he played hockey—and he played it well enough to be asked to join Britain's Olympic hockey team. He also played tennis, football and baseball impressively well.

BUT BEST OF ALL. Pearson came up with the idea for the United Nations peacekeeping force, and he was awarded the Nobel Peace Prize for his efforts. The UN peacekeepers continue to serve wherever they are needed in the world, and Canada's view of itself and its army as peacekeepers continues to bring pride to the country.

STRANGEST OF ALL? William Lyon Mackenzie King holds a couple of prime ministerial records. He was the longest-serving prime minister and he was also the strangest. King remained a bachelor all his life but had extraordinarily close relationships with a number of women. These included his neighbour's wife—and his own mother.

GOING TO THE DOGS? King led Canada throughout World War II. He frequently consulted fortune tellers and ghosts (including his mother's) for advice on how best to handle crises, and he often spoke to his dog named Pat. The dog had died some months earlier.

COMEBACK KID. The suave, debonair and controversial prime minister Pierre Elliott Trudeau announced his retirement from politics after he was defeated in 1979. The following year, though, he ran for office again—and won. He was the only prime minister to have flipped the bird to a crowd of Canadians.

NO GIRLS ALLOWED? It could seem that way, but Canada has had one female prime minister, Kim Campbell. She won the Conservative leadership after Brian Mulroney made himself more popular than he had been for years—by retiring.

OOOPS. Campbell showed an unfortunate lack of discretion in a couple of public areas. Tongues wagged when she sat for a formal photograph wearing nothing and holding her judicial robes a little south of that enigmatic smile.

PLAYING DIRTY. Another of Campbell's tactical errors was to hire an American advertising agency to help with her political campaign. Canadians were not amused when her ads mocked Jean Chretien's facial disability.

BUT, BUT, BUT. The Liberals could've fought back by focusing on Campbell's growing girth. She had complained that since taking office she had noticed a decided increase in the size of her butt! That tactic may not have been seen as very Canadian either.

AND THE WINNER IS? Not Kim. Not the Conservatives. Campbell was forced to call an election in October 1993. The Conservatives lost 153 of their 155 seats. Even Kim lost her seat.

PRIME MINISTERIAL TRIVIA

CROSSING PARTY LINES. In 1965, future prime minister John Turner saved former prime minister John Diefenbaker from drowning. They were both visiting the Barbados at the time.

PICK A COUNTRY, ANY COUNTRY. Andrew Bonar Law, a Canadian, became prime minister—of Great Britain! He served from October 1922 until May 1923. And Law's been in good company ever since. He's buried in Westminster Abbey along with other distinguished (and dead!) historical figures.

LIKE FATHER, LIKE SON. In 1891, Sir John A. Macdonald's son Hugh (also "Sir") joined his father in the House of Commons. In 1899, he became premier of Manitoba.

A DUBIOUS DISTINCTION. Canadian poet Irving Layton said of Pierre Elliott Trudeau, "He was the first prime minister of Canada worthy of assassination."

MISLEADING FIRST IMPRESSION? After meeting Adolf Hitler, William Lyon Mackenzie King decreed that the murdering mad man was "charming."

LET'S LIST LES LEADERS

Who elected these guys anyway?

SIR JOHN A. MACDONALD, CONSERVATIVE, 1867–73 AND 1878–91. Sir John Eh? once noted that Canadians would rather be led by him drunk than by his opponent sober. And apparently he was correct!

ALEXANDER MACKENZIE, LIBERAL, 1873–78. Tact clearly wasn't his strong suit! "Loyalty to the Queen does not require a man to bow down to her manservant, or her maidservant—or her ass." Mackenzie even turned down her offer to knight him—three times!

SIR JOHN ABBOTT, CONSERVATIVE, 1891–92. Apparently even Abbott thought he was a wise choice for party leader because he once said, "I am not particularly obnoxious to anybody."

SIR JOHN THOMPSON, CONSERVATIVE, 1892–94. "These Yankee politicians are the lowest race of thieves in existence." But tell us, how did you really feel, Sir John?

SIR MACKENZIE BOWELL, CONSERVATIVE, 1894–96. Unfortunately, Bowell was in a bad mood for most of his prime ministerial career. Good thing it was short-lived.

SIR CHARLES TUPPER, CONSERVATIVE, 1896. Let's hope Tupper enjoyed his stay in the prime minister's office—all ten weeks of it.

SIR WILFRID LAURIER, LIBERAL, 1896–1911. He's often credited with saying "The twentieth century belongs to Canada!" And he did say something like that. His actual words were "The nineteenth century was the century of the United States. I think we can claim that Canada will fill the twentieth century."

SIR ROBERT BORDEN, CONSERVATIVE/UNION, 1911–20.
Borden might've been a ton of fun at home, but a wag once noted that his face was "chiselled" and that he "never laughs in public."

ARTHUR MEIGHEN, CONSERVATIVE, 1920–21 AND 1926.
Needed: one dress code. Meighen once wore slippers into the House of Commons.

WILLIAM LYON MACKENZIE KING, LIBERAL, 1921–26, 1926–30, 1935–48. Long did this King reign over us, sometimes seeking advice from his mother—even many years after her death!

RICHARD B. BENNETT, CONSERVATIVE, 1930–35. Every Canadian alive during the Dirty Thirties loved to hate Prime Minister Bennett. Soon the feeling was mutual.

LOUIS ST. LAURENT, LIBERAL, 1948–57. Friends and foes alike called him "Uncle Louis." Their words may have been the same, but their tone of voice was different.

JOHN DIEFENBAKER, CONSERVATIVE, 1957–63. One of "Dief the Chief's" first successes as a young lawyer in a Saskatchewan court room came about because the jury discovered it was his birthday.

LESTER B. PEARSON, LIBERAL, 1963–68. Pearson was quite an athlete and actually played on the British hockey team in the 1920 Olympics.

PIERRE TRUDEAU, LIBERAL, 1968–79 AND 1980–84. Some found his philosophies shockingly liberal—"The state has no place in the bedrooms of the nation." Tsk!

JOE CLARK, CONSERVATIVE, 1979–80. Who could follow Trudeau and do it well? Apparently not Joe Who.

JOHN TURNER, LIBERAL, 1984. The shortest-serving PM during the 20th century. After only 80 days in office, Brian Mulroney "mopped the floor" with Turner's Liberals.

BRIAN MULRONEY, CONSERVATIVE, 1984–93. Mulroney walked into the PM's office "oozing confidence." When he left the office, Canadians were pretty uniformly oozing hate for him.

KIM CAMPBELL, CONSERVATIVE, 1993. Our only female leader didn't have much of a chance. Canadians were disgusted with her party and soundly voted them out at the first opportunity.

JEAN CHRETIEN, LIBERAL, 1993–2003. This prime minister even managed to give politicians a bad name. 'Nuff said!

PAUL MARTIN, LIBERAL, 2003–. At least Martin's been consistent in denying his involvement with "Adscam."

WORLD WARS AND COLD WAR

Lest we forget. Canada and Canadians have made enormous contributions to both world wars. In the Peace Tower at the nation's capital, the Book of Remembrance lists the names of the 111,542 men and women who were killed during the wars.

WORLD WAR I

ABOVE AND BEYOND. Canada's contribution to World War I was enormous, especially considering that becoming involved was not exactly an option. When Britain declared war on Germany, Canada was automatically drawn into the conflict. Despite this, nearly 620,000 Canadians fought—a remarkably high number considering that the entire population in 1914 was roughly 8 million.

BE PREPARED. On Easter Monday, April 9, 1917, after thousands of hours of training and preparation, Canadian soldiers attacked a rise of land in France. The assault on the Germans occupying that hill was later described as a "perfectly organized" manoeuvre. All that organization paid off in spades. Canada's soldiers succeeded where the British and French had failed. The victory at Vimy Ridge remains a galvanizing and proud military accomplishment.

A DEFINING MOMENT. The Battle of Vimy Ridge was the first time the Canadian corps had ever fought as a unit. The experience created a strong sense of patriotism for the troops, a pride that had not previously existed in the young country's history.

FLY BOY. Billy Bishop was a gutsy young man who was full of life. He loved to fly—and fight—and win. After a training period that consisted of only four hours of solo practice, Bishop began his World War I career. He was credited with shooting down 72 enemy aircraft. His raid in June 1917 earned him the Victoria Cross. A fellow flyer once said that Bishop was a "fantastic shot but a terrible pilot."

HOW UNCANADIAN. But controversy followed Billy Bishop—to the grave and beyond. More than 25 years after his death, a movie made by the National Film Board implied that Bishop had not

been nearly the hero he'd made himself out to be and that he'd either exaggerated or completely made up some of the amazing missions he reported.

A VERY CANADIAN RESPONSE. Parliament struck committees to investigate those implications, but as 65 years had passed since the events had (or hadn't!) taken place, no one could come up with a definitive answer.

WHO WAS THAT POETIC MAN? At 42, Major John McCrae, MD, was older than many of his compatriots. He was also an experienced soldier, having volunteered with the Canadian Field Artillery during the South African War. McCrae was a sensitive man who liked to express himself in both poetry and painting.

DOING HIS DUTY. John McCrae was single. He had wanted to get married, but his heart had been permanently broken. The great love of his life had died when she was still a girl. It was because he was a bachelor that McCrae felt he should join the war effort. Reasoning that he had less to lose than the married men did, he rejoined the military at the beginning of World War I.

NO MEDICAL SKILLS REQUIRED. Major McCrae was stationed in Belgium during 1915. On May 2, stretcher bearers brought in a fatally wounded Canadian, Lieutenant Alex Halmer. McCrae was devastated. Halmer had been his friend.

TRIBUTE TO A FRIEND. There was nothing that could be done for the lieutenant except to bury his remains approximately where he had fallen—among the wild poppies growing in the fields of Flanders, Belgium. The next day John McCrae wrote the poem "In Flanders Fields." Those three stanzas, originally written in his army-issue notebook, have come to symbolize Remembrance Day for Canada and much of the rest of the world.

HE TOO IS REMEMBERED. John McCrae never saw the end of "the war to end all wars." He died of pneumonia and is buried in France. In Canada, the house where McCrae lived in Guelph, Ontario, has been preserved, and a perpetual light burns to honour his memory.

SOME STILL DO THE RIGHT THING. Today, McCrae's medals are on display at that house in Guelph, thanks to the generosity of one man, Arthur Lee. Mr. Lee came to Canada with his parents when he was 12 years old. Even as an adult he knew nothing of McCrae or the medals before he attended an auction where the memorabilia was to be sold.

GOING, GOING, NOT GONE! Afraid that these small but wonderful Canadian artifacts might be bought by someone other than a Canadian, Lee outbid his nearest rival—by $100,000! After handing over a total of $400,000 for McCrae's medals, Arthur Lee then handed the medals over to the McCrae House in Guelph. Lee's act made him as much a hero in many Canadian eyes as John McCrae was already.

A BUS? One young Canadian destined to make his mark in the world was sent home from World War I to recover from injuries. No, he wasn't wounded while fighting in the trenches. Future prime minister Lester B. Pearson had been hit by a bus while he was crossing a city street in London, England.

WORLD WAR II

THE NUMBERS GAME. Roughly 1 million Canadians served in the military during World War II. Very impressive for a country with a total population of roughly 12 million.

THOSE DARING YOUNG MEN. Pilot Robert Hayward was known for his aggressive flying and fighting skills—and for his effective hits. Hayward modestly shared the credit for this success with the type of plane he flew—a Spitfire. He once explained, "You didn't fly it, you wore it like a glove and waved it around."

WATERSHED INVASION. On June 6, 1944, 110 Canadian ships carrying 14,000 Canadian soldiers landed on the beaches of Normandy, France. By the end of the day, 359 of them were dead. It was D-Day, the start of Operation Overlord. The end of World War II had begun.

MRS. DALTON'S BOYS DO THEIR PART. Elliott and Charles Dalton were among the commanding officers who led their troops onto Juno Beach in Normandy. Charles was injured in the fighting, and he was taken to the hospital. Six days later Elliott was also injured and taken to the bed beside his brother.

CAN'T KEEP A GOOD PAIR DOWN. Both Charles and Elliott recovered and returned to their positions, where they fought until victory was declared. Their valour was recognized, and they were rewarded with the Distinguished Service Order.

TIPTOE THROUGH THE TULIPS. It's May 8, 2005, the 60th anniversary of VE Day. Canadian flags flew from virtually every building in Holland. The Dutch people want the world to know how very much they appreciate the freedom that Canada's soldiers won for them.

RESPONDING TO THE CALL...AGAIN. Although they're elderly by now, many of Canada's surviving veterans travel to Holland to honour the anniversary and acknowledge the outpouring of affection the Dutch people are offering. The Canadian vets are joined by most of the leaders of the free world—except Canada's.

PETTY POLITICS. None of Canada's political leaders dared to leave their country. They were all involved in the fight of their *political* lives and afraid that treading more than a few steps from Parliament Hill would be letting their guard down. The Liberal sponsorship scandal was evidently more important to them than honouring the sacrifices and accomplishments of 60 years earlier.

THE PEOPLE SPEAK. Canadians, from ordinary citizens to decorated veterans, are outraged. They let their feelings be known and shame the political leaders into travelling to Holland to take part in the ceremonies.

WHAT'S IN A NAME? The "D" in D-Day stood for "day," so effectively June 6, 1944, was called Day-Day.

WE CAN'T GET NO RESPECT. When it was announced that the war was over, servicemen stationed in Halifax rioted and caused $1 million damage. They were angry about the lack of hospitality the city had shown them during the war.

THE GREAT ESCAPE

ARTISTIC LICENCE. The World War II movie *The Great Escape,* staring James Garner and Steve McQueen, is a classic. It tells a true story—except that because it was an American film, the prisoners are presented as Americans. However, the characters that Garner, McQueen and the other actors played never really existed. They were composites of several real-life prisoners, many of whom were Canadians.

A HERO IN THE MAKING. When World War II broke out, Wally Floody knew he had to do his part. He enlisted in the Air Force right away. When the young pilot was shot down over France in 1942, his next job was to make sure the Germans had a very difficult time keeping him.

PREVIOUS TRAINING COMES IN HANDY. Before the war, Floody had worked as a miner in northern Ontario. Little did he know what ideal training all that underground digging would prove to be, for Floody and others painstakingly dug a tunnel—9 metres underground and over 100 metres long.

A LIFESAVER. The guards at the prison camp may have become suspicious that some sort of breakout was planned. They transferred Floody and other prisoners to another camp just before the actual escape. On the night of the escape, nearly 80 prisoners crawled along the tunnel that the former miner had helped to dig. Tragically, only three of them actually made it to safety.

A SANITY SAVER TOO. Despite those terrible odds, it's likely that concentrating on their tunnelling plan helped to keep many of the prisoners, including Floody, sane while they were being held in the camp.

JUST DOING MY JOB. Floody survived the war, returned to Canada and started a family. He lived a quiet, productive life until the early 1960s, when a Hollywood producer asked him to become a technical adviser for the movie *The Great Escape.* Once again, Wally Floody did the job he was asked to do.

A MORE ANIMATED VERSION. And without *The Great Escape,* the civilized world would be without that other cinematic classic *Chicken Run!*

DID YOU  KNOW?

FIRST NATIONS FIGHT FOR CANADA. During the first two World Wars, more than 7000 Canadian aboriginal men and women volunteered to join the Allied forces in Europe. Many served as snipers or scouts, using their traditional hunting skills. Francis Pegahmagabow, an Ojibwa from Ontario, enlisted almost as soon as World War I began. A sniper, he fought at Ypres, the Somme and Passchendaele and was the most decorated Canadian Native in that war.

TOP SECRET

PSST, WANNA ENROL IN A SPY SCHOOL? Come to Canada. We have one of the best in the business. This isn't what you'd normally think of as a great way to use 105 hectares of prime southern Ontario farmland, right? But this is now and that was then—1941. World War II was raging. The allies needed to train spies, and Camp X was created.

YOUR FIRST ASSIGNMENT—MAKE SURE NO ONE FINDS IT.
The Americans chose a low-profile site between Whitby and Oshawa. It was accessible by water and close to the United States, but not so close that the enemy might think of looking there. Then, just to ensure that no one broke into the place, it was also heavily guarded.

SPIES EXTRAORDINAIRE. Actors Cary Grant and David Niven trained there, as did future prime minister Lester B. Pearson. Legend has it that Ian Fleming, creator of James Bond, was also an alumnus and that the inside information in the 007 books came from the author's days at the spy school. There's even speculation that Bond's boss, "M," was modelled after William Stephenson, a man Winston Churchill called Intrepid.

NOW THAT'S COLD. In the early 1940s, a new boathouse appeared on the shores of Patricia Lake in the Rocky Mountains near Jasper, Alberta. Well, okay, a new boathouse *seemed* to appear. In fact, it was not really a boat*house* at all. It was a boat, and a good-sized one at that. But this wasn't an ordinary boat. It was a boat made entirely of ice.

SHHH! This boat had a tin roof stuck on it as a disguise. It's not that the owners didn't want all the neighbours to know about their strange new boat. The secrecy was a matter of international security, for this bizarre craft was only a prototype. A prototype that Allied leaders hoped would help win the war.

MODEL SHIP. At a conference in Québec City, Lord Mountbatten, chief of Combined Operations, announced his plan to build huge ice ships. They would serve as platforms for both troops and airplanes. But as this was going to be a pretty darned expensive undertaking, he ordered that a trial ship should be built first.

NEXT PROJECT? By the time the prototype was floating on Patricia Lake, the ice ship idea had been abandoned, and everyone pretty much forgot about the whole outrageous, top secret idea. That is until scuba divers accidentally came across the site in the 1970s. Now that wild and crazy piece of Canadian war history is proudly acknowledged with a plaque.

BROKEN ARROW

TRUE OR FALSE? A live nuclear bomb lay on Canadian soil for some four years.

AND THE ANSWER IS... Hate to tell you this, but the likely answer is "True." In all probability, America's first Broken Arrow, the U.S. military's code for a lost atomic bomb, lay on a mountainside in northern British Columbia for four years! Sound like a modern myth? No such luck. Read on.

NICE DAY FOR A CLIMB. In 1954, a mountaineer from Smithers, British Columbia, was hired to guide a group of Americans on a treacherous trek. The group needed to get to a remote site near the top of a nearby mountain as quickly as possible.

WHO WERE THESE HURRIED PEOPLE? These weren't just ordinary, curious folks wanting to climb a Canadian mountain. These were members of the United States military on a top secret expedition.

ONE OF OUR BOMBS IS MISSING. The American government had just received word that a mountain climber had found the wreckage of an aircraft—an aircraft that had crashed about midnight on February 13, 1950. For 48 months, the world, the U.S. military included, had mistakenly believed that the missing plane had crashed into the Pacific Ocean.

A SLIGHT MISCALCULATION. But the wreck wasn't in a reasonably safe resting place at the bottom of the ocean after all. It was on land. Considering the crashed plane had been carrying an atomic weapon, that made a big difference.

AND THEN...? Once the members of the special team arrived on the mountaintop, they worked quickly—and explosively. First they attended to a few of those pesky housekeeping matters, like deactivating the bomb's core. Next they blew what was left of the crashed plane to smithereens. Their work there was done. All that remained was to get safely back home and keep their mouths shut about what they'd done and why they'd done it.

MISSION UNCOVERED. Their secret might have been safe except that a small and very curious group of men was determined to find out what actually happened on that mountainside so long ago. In 2003, these men flew to the crash site at their own expense. Three days later they came away convinced that for four years there had been a live nuclear weapon lying on the side of a mountain in northern British Columbia.

NO ONE TALKS. The U.S. military still won't say anything about whether or not there was a live atomic bomb aboard that original flight. Nor will they say anything about why they sent in the cleanup crew. Was it a cover-up? Those who know most about the crash think it is.

AND NOW? Today there's a law protecting the crash site from looters. Despite this, determined treasure hunters still make their way up the mountain to see where the world's first Broken Arrow once lay.

NUMBER TWO. Nine months after that plane hit the mountain, another American plane, also carrying an atomic weapon, ran into trouble near Rimouski, Québec. The crew managed to drop the bomb into the St. Lawrence River. It exploded, scattering a few kilograms of uranium, but the plutonium core was missing, so luckily, there was no mushroom cloud.

WAITING FOR THE BIG ONE?

One of the kookiest places in Canada definitely has one of the kookiest histories. But it's not on Canadian soil. It's in Canadian soil. What else could it be but the Diefenbunker? If your reaction is "the Diefenwhatsit?" chances are you were born after the Cold War ended.

THE BIG CHILL. In 1959, when the Cold War was getting frosty, paranoia was rampant. Many Canadians citizens built underground rooms where they thought they would be safe in case of a nuclear war (or "nucular" if you're listening to President George W. Bush).

IF THE PEOPLE LEAD, THE LEADERS WILL FOLLOW. From 1959 to 1961 Diefenbaker's Conservative government sank (literally) a lot of money into a building in (again, literally) Carp, ON, near Ottawa.

YOU COULDN'T MAKE THIS STUFF UP. The building was called the Central Emergency Government Headquarters, but was nick-named the Diefenbunker. It's a four-storey building that goes down *into* the ground. This subterranean office building, with living quarters for VIPs, is one of the strangest legacies of the Cold War.

GET DOWN! Fortunately underground Ottawa, as it might have been called, never had to be used. Despite this, the place was maintained until 1994. Today, the Diefenbunker is a National Historic Site.It's a museum that's not only open to the public, but actually attracts visitors. The place is outrageously popular.

TALK ABOUT YOUR CLEVER USE OF SPACE. Today Canadians can tour the Diefenbunker.What's more, the museum offers movie nights and specially chosen guest speakers. Kids can go to "spy camp" underground, there are scavenger hunts, midnight tours, backroom tours and even ghost tours on Halloween.

WHO WAS THAT MASKED MAN?

THE SPY WHO CAME IN FROM THE COLD. During World War II, the Allies were spying on the enemy and vice versa. That meant there were (gasp!) spies in Canada.

COME ON HOME. Of course, once the war was over there wasn't much need for the services of those spies, and one by one they were called home. When Russian spy Igor Gouzenko received word that the Soviets wanted him back on home turf, he didn't react well. He'd been living in our nation's capital for some years and had become quite fond of the place.

I DON'T WANNA GO! The thought of leaving Canada, especially to go back to Russia, was decidedly unappealing to Gouzenko. But what could he do? After considerable thought, the man came up with a devious idea. He would steal documents from the Soviet embassy, where he had been working.

PAPER PROOF. Igor chose the documents he would steal with great care. He wanted to make sure the Canadian government knew just how dastardly the Russians had been and that he had absolutely turned against his homeland. By September 6, 1945, he had gathered quite a stack of papers.

HERE GOES! Igor Gouzenko tucked the evidence under his jacket and, trying not to look nervous, left the Soviet embassy for the last time.

HOW CANADIAN. Despite all his preparation, Gouzenko discovered it wasn't so simple for a spy to retire. He went directly to the offices of the *Ottawa Journal* and plunked every one of those Russian spy documents down on a reporter's desk. You'd think it would be a dream come true for any journalist, but the reporter told him to pack up his papers and take them to the RCMP.

AND THEN...? For some reason, instead of going to the RCMP, Gouzenko went to the Department of Justice—which by that time was closed for the day. Poor Igor. He was terrified, and with good reason. If the Russians got wind of what he'd done and what he was trying to do, his life would be worth nothing. Worse, his family wouldn't be safe either.

AT LAST. The next morning Gouzenko packed up his papers and tried his luck at the newspaper one more time. Finally someone gave the man the attention he'd been craving.

GOOD NEWS, BAD NEWS. By noon the Canadian government had found out about the spy and the pile of goodies he'd taken with him from Russia's embassy. That was finally a bit of good news for Gouzenko. But there was bad news too. The Russian government had also found out what he'd done—and the Russians were after him.

BREAK IN! He knew he wouldn't be safe in his home that night, so he took his wife and children to a friend's place. They weren't safe there either. Russian officials found them. Fortunately, the family that had taken the Gouzenkos in called the city police, who called the RCMP, who in turn called the Canadian government, which called off the Russians. Finally, the man's nightmare was over.

WITNESS PROTECTION PROGRAM. Gouzenko and his family were safe. The daring spy who had been so determined to stay in Canada did get his wish. The government supplied him with a new identity, and he went about his life as normally as he could.

PILLOWCASE DISGUISE. Whenever he had to appear as his former self—the Russian traitor—Gouzenko put a hood over his head. The disguise looked for all the world like a pillowcase with two slits cut into it for eye holes. He even wore it when he was the mystery guest on the popular Canadian television show *Front Page Challenge.*

CAREER CHANGE. Gouzenko soon wrote and published his autobiography. Then he went on to write a novel which won the Governor General's award. He died in 1982.

THE SPY ON THE WET COAST. In 1965, Cold War paranoia reached its peak. Vancouver resident George Victor Spencer was charged with "low-level spying" (something like being a "little bit" pregnant?). To assure Canadians that matters were well in hand, it was reported that Spencer was at home but under constant surveillance.

WAY TO WATCH 'EM, BOYS! Spencer's body was found in his kitchen on April 9, 1966. Officials determined that he'd been dead for three days. Guess there must be a number of ways to define the term "constant surveillance."

PLAINS, TRAINS, CAMELS...

Canadians have travelled over, through, and around their great country using many different modes of transportation.

PUT A SPIKE IN IT, BOYS

Right from the start, Canadian politicians realized that the enormous size of this country could work to its disadvantage. So as quickly as they could, they connected us from sea to sea with a ribbon of steel.

NICE DAY FOR A GET-TOGETHER. On November 7, 1885 (just days before Louis Riel was hanged, but that's a whole other story), the biggest Canadian bigwigs milled around at the side of the railway tracks in the little town of Craigellachie, British Columbia. If you'd asked them, they no doubt would have told you that they were there to see the "last spike" driven into the cross-Canada rail line.

WATCH THE BIRDIE! But they'd have been lying, as Canadian politicians have been known to do the odd time. Those hoary old men were really there for the photo-op. Even then everyone knew that this would be a history-making occasion. And they were right about that, weren't they? Because we've all seen the photograph that was taken that day.

MONEY SWINGS. The man in the photo who is actually swinging the hammer to pound in the last spike is Donald Smith, a.k.a. the future Lord Strathcona. It was fitting that Smith should have been given this honour, as he financed many miles of the railway.

A PICTURE IS WORTH A THOUSAND WORDS, *BUT* BEHIND EVERY PICTURE THERE'S A STORY. Prime Minister Sir John A. Macdonald was also there for the last spike ceremony. Now, Macdonald and Smith did not like one another—at all. Smith thought Macdonald was a corrupt politician, which was an absolutely accurate opinion, but Macdonald didn't think Smith should have told everyone about those pesky bribes going through the prime minister's office.

BENT OUT OF SHAPE I. As the photographer was making sure that everyone said "cheese" at exactly the right moment, Macdonald was seething with anger that Smith had grabbed the best pose and position for the picture.

BENT OUT OF SHAPE II. As it turned out, Smith didn't do a very good job pounding in that last spike. The big nail didn't actually go in—it bent. Never mind. A trackmaster named Brothers handed the lord another spike and the deed was finally done.

NOT ALL SPIKES ARE CREATED EQUAL. It's a good thing the wise men had decided against using the special silver spike that had been cast for the occasion. It would've been a shame to have bent that one!

SAFETY FIRST. The silver spike wasn't used because authorities feared souvenir hunters might try to pry it out. Then the track wouldn't be safe.

WHERE DID IT GO? That symbolic silver spike was eventually mounted on a marble base, and then...it disappeared. Its whereabouts are still a mystery today. Some people think that it became a family heirloom for the descendants of William Cornelius Van Horne.

VAN WHO? William Cornelius Van Horne was president of the Canadian Pacific Railway. He was also a man of amazing energy. He ran the railroad, but he also worked physically right alongside the labourers who were building the line. He once referred to himself as the "boss of everybody and everything."

SOME WORKERS ARE MORE EQUAL THAN OTHERS. Of course, at the end of the day Van Horne dined elegantly on sumptuous food in luxurious surroundings, while the labourers returned to their lodgings to eat what was available.

ONE HUMP OR TWO?

Money, money, money—the love of it might be the root of all evil, but trying to get rich can certainly help a person think "creatively."

PROFIT MOTIVES WE UNDERSTAND. Successful gold mining is a rewarding endeavour, well worth some innovative effort. During the 1860s, thousands of wannabe miners hoped that the Cariboo Gold Rush would be their road to reward. Unfortunately, most of them didn't foresee just how rough that road was going to be.

THAT'S A LONG WAY DOWN! The creek sides that hid the precious nuggets were steep—really steep. Pack horses and mules had been useful in both the Alaska and the California gold rushes, but those animals were having a pretty tough time on the terrain of British Columbia's Cariboo Mountains.

WHAT ROCKET SURGEON THOUGHT OF THIS? One clever miner was sure he had the answer. It was so simple. Why hadn't anyone thought of it before? Camels! Of course, camels were the obvious solution. Weren't they? All they had to do was ship camels from the deserts of the Middle East! And they did.

BUT WAIT, HERE'S A REAL SURPRISE! The imported beasts weren't very useful. As a matter of fact, the entire experiment failed miserably.

PAW-LICKING GOOD. The miners were disappointed. They weren't, however, heavily into the compassionate care of displaced animals. They simply turned the camels loose. And that is how a herd of wild camels came to be roaming in western Canada for some 40 years. It is also how local wolves and bears developed a taste for imported meat.

HIGH-FLYING HISTORY

*But let's not content ourselves with getting around by train
—let's hit some highs too! And, sadly, some lows.*

WHAT A DAY! On February 20, 1959, Prime Minister John
Diefenbaker rose in Parliament and announced that work on the
Avro Arrow, a supersonic interceptor jet, was over. In one sen-
tence, Canada's place in world aviation history was permanently
damaged and 14,000 Canadian workers were out of work.

OUR LOSS, THEIR GAIN. There was an upside to all of this, but
unfortunately not for Canada. Officials from America's space
program immediately dropped what they'd been doing and flew
north. They hired as many engineers from the Arrow project as
they possibly could. Those suddenly unemployed Canadians
helped the United States win the space race.

BUT WHY? Diefenbaker claimed that finances were behind his
decision to abandon the Arrow, but that explanation didn't fly
with Canadians. Even today, almost 50 years later, the decision
remains controversial.

WHAT A SAVE! Wilfrid was an inexperienced but gutsy young
Canadian pilot in World War I. And for a few fatal moments it
looked as though that was all he was ever going to be. The deadly
Red Baron had him in his sights. Seconds later the enemy plane
had been blown to bits.

DID HE OR DIDN'T HE? Wilfrid's old school friend Captain
Roy Brown was credited with saving his life by killing the deadly
German flying ace. Today there's some debate about whether
Brown shot down the plane, but the important point is that

Wilfrid did not become the Red Baron's 81st kill. Instead, Wilfrid "Wop" May went on to greatness.

ANOTHER GREAT SAVE. On New Year's Day, 1929, the people in the northern Alberta community of Fort Vermillion needed medication. An epidemic of diphtheria threatened to ravage their tiny village. The area was usually reached by dogsled, but even the most efficient team would take two weeks to reach them, and the people simply could not hold out that long.

ONLY YOU. Clearly, Wop May was the man for the job. May and co-pilot Vic Horner flew a 75-horsepower plane with an open cockpit almost 1000 kilometres in sub-zero temperatures and blizzard conditions. They were so cold by the time they reached their destination that they had to be pried from their seats.

HOMETOWN HEROES! Their mission was a success and an enormous crowd of admirers was on hand for their return home to Edmonton.

AND THEN...? Three years later, Wop May made history—and headlines—once again by using his skills as a pilot to help track and capture an outlaw. Albert Johnson, better known as the Mad Trapper, had killed a Mountie. The dead man's colleagues were determined to catch and punish the murderer. May's involvement from the air was the first time a plane had ever been used in a manhunt.

OLDIES, BUT NOT GOODIES. Remember, you read it here first. The Sea King helicopters owned and flown by Canada's armed forces were state-of-the-art machines—more than 40 years ago!

IS IT A BIRD? IS IT A PLANE? Canada was the third country to put a satellite into orbit. We successfully launched the *Alouette* in 1962.

CUNARDLY WAIT TO GO TO SEA

LIKE FATHER, LIKE SON. Samuel Cunard was born in Halifax and followed his father into Canada's early timber business, sort of. By the early 1830s, this War of 1812 veteran had become a boat builder. Okay, maybe "shipping magnate" would describe the situation better.

GOOD KNIGHT. By the time Cunard died in 1865, he had been knighted in recognition of the support he gave to the British Empire during the Crimean War. And he was extremely wealthy. The Cunard line remains a big player in the world's shipping industry.

I MUST GO DOWN TO THE SEA AGAIN. In 1907, Cunard Steamship Company launched the largest, most luxurious ship the world had ever seen—the *Lusitania.* What a unique vacation for the ridiculously rich! A palatial, floating hotel! In no time at all, it seemed, the new ocean liner had become *very* popular. And what a money-maker!

ANYTHING YOU CAN DO, I CAN DO BETTER. As in any business, there was rivalry in the shipping industry. For the Cunard line, the most serious competitor was the White Star line. From the moment the *Lusitania* was launched, the market heated up. White Star knew it had to do something pretty impressive to keep its place in the shipping industry. And it did.

FIRST BEHEMOTH. White Star designed and began to build a trio of ships—the *Olympic, Titanic* and *Britannic*—so huge that any one of them made the *Lusitania* look puny. On October 20, 1910, thousands gathered to watch the first of those three mammoths, the *Olympic,* launched into glory. It wasn't until the ship's fifth voyage that the behemoth really made history.

EVERYONE'S LUCKY DAY. As it passed the navy cruiser *Hawke,* the *Olympic's* wake sucked the smaller vessel towards it until the *Hawke* smashed against the *Olympic.* It was nothing short of a miracle that no one was killed. The accident was conveniently forgotten about until April 10, 1912, that infamous date in shipping history when the *Olympic's* sister ship, the *Titanic,* began its first trans-Atlantic voyage.

SECOND BEHEMOTH. Apparently those in charge had not learned much from the near-catastrophe involving the *Hawke* and the *Olympic.* There was at least one small ship, the *New York,* nearby as the *Titanic* set off. The waves created by the huge ship ripped the smaller one from its moorings and drew it towards the *Titanic.* A metre short of disaster, a tugboat caught the *New York* and pulled it from harm's way.

GRIM. The *Titanic* sailed away into tragic infamy, killing 1522 people and changing the course of Halifax's history forever. Ships from that city were sent to recover the victims and bring them back to Halifax for identification and burial. The city's resources were stretched to their limits. Buildings became makeshift morgues; gravediggers worked overtime. Even today, the effects of the *Titanic's* sinking are felt in Halifax as thousands of visitors are drawn to pay their respects at the cemeteries where many of the victims are buried.

GRIMMER. The only ship to respond to the *Titanic's* calls for help was the *Carpathia,* which was, ironically, owned by Cunard lines. That tidbit of information could take this tale of luxury and tragedy full circle, except that in those days, wireless operators aboard ships did not work for the shipping company but for the telegraph company, and the Marconi Company, which employed the telegrapher working on *Carpathia,* ordered him to stop sending messages about the tragedy.

GRIMMEST OF ALL. It seems that news of the disaster had spread, and the Marconi Company had promised the exclusive story to the *New York Times.* And in order to show themselves in a good light, the *Titanic's* owners were spinning the disaster in a very dishonest way. They announced that everyone aboard the sinking ship had been successfully rescued. Of course, that couldn't have been further from the truth.

DAMN THE TORPEDOS! But what of the *Lusitania?* The Cunard ship that started the outlandish race to be the biggest and most prestigious shipping line in the world left New York harbour on May 1, 1915. World War I raged. The *Lusitania's* captain could see the shores of Ireland when his ship was torpedoed by a German submarine. Nearly 1200 people were killed.

IRONY OF IRONIES. In 1934, Cunard absorbed the White Star Line.

GRUESOME DISTINCTION. In the wee hours of May 29, 1914, on the St. Lawrence River, near Rimouski, Québec, the *Empress of Ireland* earned its terrible place in history as the worst-ever Canadian shipping disaster. The *Empress* went down fast, just 14 minutes after being T-boned by a coal carrier. The ship took 1014 souls with it. Some folks likely never even woke up in time to know they were drowning.

CURSES ON YOU. The world remains fascinated by the *Titanic's* demise, but the story of the *Empress* is virtually unknown. That's strange, considering the marvellously convoluted curse theory associated with it.

QUACK, QUACK. Hawley Harvey Crippen liked to call himself Dr. Crippen. The title no doubt improved his standing in the community, but in reality the man was little more than a quack. He was a natty dresser and imagined himself quite the ladies' man. As we join Crippen's story, it is 1910. He and his second wife are living in marital disharmony.

WILL THAT BE ARSENIC OR STRYCHNINE? Crippen soon found a deadly solution to his marital difficulties—one containing poison. Once his wife had breathed her last, he cut her body up and hid the bits under their house. Then Crippen boarded a ship—the SS *Montrose*. It was heading for Canada.

TOUGH BREAK, DOC. Poor Crippen, if it weren't for bad luck, he wouldn't have had any luck at all. He was soon found out. The *Montrose* was equipped with one of those newfangled Marconi devices, and the ship's captain—a man named Kendall—was made aware that one of his passengers was wanted in connection with a murder in England. Kendall contacted the authorities.

GOTCHA! Soon a pilot boat appeared alongside the *Montrose*. The captain of the smaller craft was a man named Belanger. His passenger was Chief Constable McCarthy. Together they boarded the *Montrose* and arrested Crippen. The natty murderer was furious. He screamed at Captain Kendall, "You will suffer for this." Before the year was out, Crippen had been hanged.

TOO COINCIDENTAL TO BE A COINCIDENCE? Four years later, at almost the same spot on the St. Lawrence where Crippen had been arrested, the *Empress of Ireland* sank. Kendall was the captain, and he went down with his ship.

GRISLY COINCIDENCE. The captain of the first boat on the scene was the man who had been in charge of the pilot boat carrying Chief Constable McCarthy, Crippen's arresting officer. And

McCarthy himself was assigned to guard the ship carrying the coffins of the *Empress's* victims. If that wasn't Crippen's curse at work, then there certainly were a lot of connections between the two events.

THE PLAY'S THE THING. In 1961, two playwrights, who hopefully exhibited more writing skill than taste, produced a musical about the Crippen murder case. It closed in just six weeks. Perhaps that's more a reflection of the audience's basic good taste than an indication the curse was still active.

DID YOU  KNOW?

BEARING GIFTS. Like all good tourists, the Viking explorers who came to Canada took home souvenirs. Their choice of gifts was pretty daring: live polar bears. That tidbit suggests *way* more questions than it answers! How did they catch the bears? How did they ship them home? The answer to both is probably "very carefully!"

ODDS 'N ENDS

Here are some quirky Canadian historical facts that will tickle your funny bone and make you go hmm...

FIRSTS

Hurry, hurry, hurry! Don't forget
—whether a thing is good or bad, it's best to be first!!

NOW WE'RE COOKING. A very small piece of Canadian history was made in Ottawa during 1891. That was when and where electricity was first used to cook food.

UP, UP AND AWAY! On September 29, 1962, Canada became the first country (okay, the first other than the United States and the Soviet Union!) to launch a satellite into space. It was named *Alouette*.

YOU'VE COME A VERY LONG WAY. In 1989, Deanna Brasseur and Jane Foster, both members of Canada's armed forces, made history by becoming the world's first female jet fighter pilots.

HOW RUDE. Pierre Elliott Trudeau was the first prime minister to flip Canadians "the bird."

EVEN RUDER. Matthew Baillie Begbie served in a rougher time—the Cariboo Gold Rush. Begbie, British Columbia's first judge, was known far and wide as "the Hanging Judge." He even threatened to have an entire jury hanged once. It's no wonder he wasn't popular, but probably he didn't know just how unpopular he was until he overheard a plan to assassinate him.

THE JUDGE FIGHTS BACK. Begbie responded by dumping his chamber pot on the would-be murderers. Not only was he not assassinated, but by 1870 he had been named British Columbia's first chief justice.

A CHANGE IS AS GOOD AS AN INCORPORATION THEY ALWAYS SAY. On May 18, 1785, Parr Town in New Brunswick changed its name to Saint John and became Canada's first incorporated city. Remember, you read it here first!

How It All Began. Exporting lumber has been important to the Canadian economy since 1785. That's when William Davidson began selling tree trunks from his homestead on the Miramichi River. The Royal Navy was his best customer. They paid a whopping $680 for masts for their ships.

Nice Ride. By 1790, rafts of timber were routinely put together and floated downstream to market. Lumberjacks went along for the ride. They built shacks on the rafts and lived on board as the logs travelled. Sort of an early-day houseboat!

Quakes Alive! Canada's first recorded earthquake shook things up in 1638. But the quake in 1663, near Québec City, was a real bell-ringer. There was no Richter scale to measure the actual force, but settlers' descriptions are almost as useful. "Buildings split asunder…mountains seemed to move…trees were uprooted." But, what scared them most of all was that in churches, "the bells rang without being touched."

First New Year's Baby? The first non-Native child to be born on Canadian soil was likely a baby Viking. The baby's last name is variously spelled Thorbandsson, Thorfinnesson and Thorfinnsson, but given that the little boy's first name was Snorri, it probably doesn't matter. The blessed event occurred circa 1000.

Send in the Clowns. Too bad little Snorri couldn't have waited till the first circus came. In 1798, the Ricketts Company's clowns and trained animal acts sailed from London, England, and put on a show in Québec City.

THE FIRST GLOBE. In 1507, a German mapmaker drew an amazing map of the entire world—as he knew it. The map consisted of a dozen wedge-shaped pieces of paper. The pieces were intended to be stuck onto a small wooden ball. That would've created *(drum roll here, please)*...the world's first globe.

THERE WE ARE! Martin Waldseemuller drew the map based on information that Christopher Columbus, John Cabot and others had brought back from their travels. It shows one of the first depictions of Canada—sort of. South America is apparently identifiable below "a series of smaller, unrecognizable land masses, reaching about 60 degrees north latitude." The last part of that description refers to Canada.

GOING, GOING, GONE. Staff at Canada's national archives would have liked to bid on this map when it came up for sale. Sadly, they were a little short of funds to meet the $2 million price tag. Oh well, someone wealthier will get to keep the first picture of Canada.

DIG THAT! Early settlers on the Canadian prairie often built their first homes from clumps of sod—usually 50 tonnes of the stuff!

DO YOU HEAR WHAT I HEAR? Reginald Fessenden was such a thoughtful inventor—not surprising for a Canadian. On Christmas Eve, 1906, he broadcast music to ships on the Atlantic Ocean. Until then, only Morse code had been transmitted over the wireless.

DO YOU SEE WHAT I SEE? In 1535, Jacques Cartier made his way up the St. Lawrence River to what today is Montréal. There he found a well-established farming village that the Natives called Hochelaga. Fortunately, Cartier took good notes while he was there because he was the first and only European to ever see the place.

OOPS! Cartier managed to offend the Natives, so on his next trip he avoided going near Hochelaga. It wasn't until 1603 that the French visited the Montréal area again, and by that time there was no trace of Hochelaga. Presumably an archeological dig under Montréal would turn up the lost village.

DID YOU  KNOW?

REFORMED SINNERS ARE USUALLY THE WORST. We all know that Sir John A. Macdonald, Canada's first prime minister, had a great fondness for liquor, but did you know that later in life he gave up drinking entirely and actually supported the temperance movement?

OLD SOBER-SIDES. Did you know that Alexander Mackenzie, Canada's second prime minister, was an abstainer? Coincidence, or had the voters become more sober about who they were voting into office?

HE SAID, SHE SAID...

Sometimes what you say depends on where you stand!

VOLTAIRE ON CANADA. Those dead French philosophers can get such a bad rap, can't they? Everyone thinks that when Voltaire heard that Canada had been reclaimed by the British, he scoffed that the loss to France wasn't important anyway because Canada was only "a few acres of snow."

VOLTAIRE, CALL YOUR LAWYER! But Voltaire has been misquoted—constantly and consistently—for 300 years! His actual words were "[England and France] have been fighting over a few acres of snow *near* Canada." He was actually referring to the Maritimes, or Acadia as it was called then. So now everyone in Canada, except Maritimers of course, can like Voltaire again.

AMERICANS ON CANADA. "Push on, brave boys. Québec is ours," American general Richard Montgomery assured his troops on New Year's Eve, 1775. Unfortunately for the good general's credibility, the attack was not successful.

HE GOT THAT WRONG. President Thomas Jefferson assured his troops that victory over Canada "would be a mere matter of marching." Unfortunately, for the man's reliability as a military prognosticator, the Americans lost the War of 1812.

THE PRAIRIE? USELESS DESERT? Fieldwork has sometimes been necessary to dispel lies about Canada. Alexander Galt, one of the Fathers of Confederation, had been told that the Canadian prairie was a "useless desert." He travelled to southern Alberta and was so impressed with what he found there that he contradicted the detractors, telling potential settlers, "Don't you believe them. This land will one day support a great population." Galt proved his own theory by prospering in southern Alberta.

THEM'S FIGHTING WORDS. By 1775, the 13 American colonies were getting very tired of having their every move controlled by Britain. They decided to rebel against this domination. One of the leaders of their revolt declared, "Canada must be demolished."

NICE TO MEET YOU. When Sir Isaac Brock met Tecumseh, the great Shawnee chief proclaimed of the British leader, "This is a man." Tecumseh was a pretty darned astute observer.

WORDS TO LIVE BY. It's tough to argue the effectiveness of suffragette Nellie McClung's recipe for action. "Never retreat, never explain, never apologize—get the thing done and let them howl."

WE'LL VOTE WITH OUR FEET. In 1913, Nellie McClung met with Manitoba's Premier Rodmond Roblin. She was there to convince the provincial leader that women should be allowed to vote. Maybe he was trying to put McClung in her place when he replied that "nice" women didn't want to vote. "Nice" try, Mr. Roblin!

THE FUTURE IS NOW. Irene Parlby, a suffragette colleague of McClung, declared, "The day has forever fled when the woman can confine her interests within the four walls of her home."

THE CANADIAN HYSTERICAL, ER...HISTORICAL SOCIETY

Canadian history has such a bad rep. Everyone says it's boring. Maybe there are boring parts to it, but there are also some pretty neat stories sprinkled throughout.

PSSSSST, WANNA BUY A MONEY PIT? The owners of Nova Scotia's Oak Island, with its possible buried riches, have officially given up the treasure hunt. Dan Blankenship and David Tobias are the latest in a 200-year-long line of people who have devoted their lives to finding the booty that *might* be buried on the tiny island—and failed.

WHAT'S UNDER THERE? The Oak Island mystery has driven people mad since 1795, when three boys discovered a carefully reinforced shaft hidden near an old oak tree. Six people have died trying to solve the mystery. Depending on which legend you read, the pit is variously believed to be where Captain Kidd stashed his plunder, Marie Antoinette's lost jewels, the Holy Grail, profits from piracy, or...?

LET ME BACK IN—I'M SUPPOSED TO BE YOUR LEADER! As a young man, Franklin Delano Roosevelt loved to spend at least part of every summer on Campobello Island in New Brunswick. In 1921, Roosevelt developed polio while he was in Canada. When he tried to return to the United States, border officials would not let him leave the Canadian side of the border.

LET'S THINK ABOUT THIS. Finally, the powers that be made an exception and let Roosevelt go home. A dozen years later he became the American president. The history of both countries might otherwise have been quite different!

BOOZE AND BIRTH CONTROL. Dr. Elizabeth Bagshaw's life was remarkable for its length alone. She lived past her 100th birthday. During those hundred years she altered the course of history for many Canadian women by providing them with reliable birth control. Bagshaw was an early feminist, and to be a feminist in that era also meant endorsing the temperance movement.

CRIMINALLY CHARMING. In the early 1920s, when Prohibition reigned, Elizabeth Bagshaw admitted a grudging appreciation for Rocco Perri, known as "the king of the bootleggers." He once escorted her from a house that was about to be raided for illegal booze, where she had been proselytizing. She happily reported that she found the kingpin criminal to be "gentlemanly."

QUITE A PAIR! Bagshaw also noted that she and Perri were in similar lines of work. At the time, distributing liquor and distributing birth control information were both criminal activities. Distributing booze became legal again in 1927. But distributing information on birth control remained illegal until 1969, when Prime Minister Pierre Trudeau decreed that the state had no place in the nation's bedrooms!

LET HIM EAT CAKE—BUT NOT HERE. World-renowned scientist Dr. David Suzuki, wearing jeans and a sports shirt, showed up at the House of Commons restaurant for a luncheon he'd been invited to. The maitre d' refused to let him in because his clothes didn't meet the dress code.

LET'S GET CONSISTENT HERE. Suzuki was surprised and pointed out that he'd eaten there just the week before. The maitre d' explained that they'd abandoned the dress-code rules on that day because there had been a meeting of aboriginal people. He had assumed that Suzuki, who is of Japanese heritage, was part of that group.

A QUIET PROFIT MOTIVE. In the early 1900s, New Brunswick tycoon K.C. Irving was just a boy. For a time he kept ducks as pets. Soon the people living near his parents complained about the noise the ducks made. The future multi-millionaire began his career that day. He had the animals slaughtered and then sold them to the very neighbours who'd complained in the first place.

FROM THOSE HUMBLE BEGINNINGS... It was a prophetic moment. Irving had solved the problem, so the neighbours were happy. And he had made money, so he was happy. Canada's first entrepreneurial industrialist had made his first deal.

GASP! NOT IN TORONTO THE GOOD! Publisher Jack McClelland of McClelland & Stewart was better known for his unconventional behaviour than for his sobriety. In 1980, he arranged a toga party to launch a book called *The Emperor's Virgin.* McClelland and the book's author, Sylvia Fraser, made history by being the first, and last, people to drive a chariot down Toronto's Yonge Street—while wearing white sheets as togas.

WEATHERING THE SPIRITS. A good old Canadian blizzard made modesty difficult and encouraged comments that Jack McClelland was slowing down. For that launch, people noted, he was "only one sheet to the wind."

SOMEONE HAD TO DO IT. Joey Smallwood led Newfoundland into Confederation in 1949 and then remained as the province's leader until 1972. In 1968, he made history by being the first person to render the always-eloquent Prime Minister Pierre Trudeau speechless.

TOO MUCH INFORMATION. In the middle of a political conversation, Smallwood asked, "Do you ever cry, Mr. Trudeau?" Predictably, there was an awkward pause. Then the premier continued by revealing that he cried "every day."

ALL IN THE FAMILY. Daniel Johnson was elected premier of Québec in 1966. His son Pierre-Marc Johnson became Québec's premier in 1985, and his other son, Daniel, took the position in 1993 and 1994.

DOES IT GET MORE PERFECTLY CANADIAN THAN THIS? According to David Phillips, Environment Canada's senior climatologist, i.e., the guy who should know, "the first official weather observation was made on the grounds of King's College, University of Toronto by the British Royal Artillery" on September 6, 1840.

WEATHER OR NOT. It took another 31 years (and an injection of $5000 in government money) before Ottawa began to provide weather information services to average Canadians.

REACH FOR THE BUTTON. The quiz show, that standard of radio and television programming, was invented by a Canadian. Before the Depression, Roy Dickson taught school in Toronto. He liked to ask his students questions that would show off the knowledge he'd helped them gain. The game was so popular with the students that Dickson thought other people might also enjoy playing.

NOW THAT CAUGHT ON! He managed to attract three sponsors, and on May 15, 1935, *Professor Dick and his Question Box* went on the air. Within two years there were more than 200 quiz shows in the world patterned after *Professor Dick*.

LIES THAT WOULD (OR SHOULD) NOT DIE

Canadians are such honest folks, aren't they? Well, sometimes they are, and other times...at least they mean well.

WHO GOT HERE FIRST? We now know that the Vikings landed on Canadian shores by the year 1000. But until the 1960s, when the ruins of their settlement at L'Anse aux Meadows, Newfoundland, was found, that fact was thought to have been only a legend.

REALLY? It's difficult to knock that initial cynicism when you consider there was also a legend that an Irish monk sailed to Canada's eastern shores, where he said Mass on the back of a whale after seeing monsters and mermaids.

OOPS, SORRY KIDS! High-school students in Ontario during the 1940s were taught that sometime around the year 1000, Norse warriors had explored the land near Lake Nipigon. Why, it even said so in the history textbooks! The only problem was that the "fact" was based on a hoax; a widely believed hoax, but a hoax nonetheless.

THEY'RE THE REAL THING! It seems that two men, Fletcher Gell and J.E. Dodd, claimed that they had found the remains of a Norse sword, an axe head and a shield grip buried beside a railway line near Beardmore, Ontario. The relics were examined by experts and found to be authentic.

A SCAM OF EPIC PROPORTIONS. The Royal Ontario Museum proudly displayed the pieces for nearly 20 years, until 1957, when the scam was revealed for what it was. Thieves had hidden the relics by the railway tracks after stealing them from a home they had burglarized.

MORE LIES? In 1882, prospectors near Cassiar, British Columbia, found more than they bargained for—coins! But not just any coins—Chinese coins circa 2000 BC! Surely the money *must* have been dropped by another miner who'd had it as a keepsake, except that anthropologists do believe there were periods when Mongolians, Koreans, Japanese and yes, even Chinese people migrated to North America.

HIS RECORDS. Chinese explorer Hoei Shin may have been referring to the coast of British Columbia when he described "the Great Land of Rushing Waters." He noted with evident interest that the people he found living there seemed peaceful and didn't have any need of fortifications.

THEIR RECORDS. The history of the Natives on and near the shores of British Columbia includes references to strange visitors who appeared before James Cook arrived. The Nuu-chah-nulth called these people "The Eaters of Maggots"—likely rice. And there is another possible piece of evidence that the Chinese influenced West Coast culture. The Nuu-chah-nulth's traditional hat is similar to that of the Chinese prior to the 18th century.

TRUTH? CONSEQUENCES? Others go so far as to maintain that evidence of an early Japanese culture has been found in British Columbia. And it's tough to argue with the ancient Japanese sword unearthed by road builders in Nanaimo on Vancouver Island—unless those kidders from Beardmore, Ontario, have been at it again!

LET'S PLAY NICELY TOGETHER. Donnacona was chief of the Iroquois village Stadacona during the era of Jacques Cartier's trips from France to the New World. At first the two men got along together famously. The Iroquois even taught the French how to prevent scurvy, the deadly disease that had killed so many of Cartier's men.

AN EARLY KIDNAPPING. Cartier probably soured those French-Native relations considerably, though, when he kidnapped Donnacona and his two sons, along with seven others, and took them back to France so that the king could see these exotic people.

NEVER KID A KIDDER. Donnacona told the King of France about a marvellous place just beyond the land that Cartier had explored. Saguenay was a kingdom of fabulous riches, the kidnapped man explained. He offered to show Cartier this wondrous land. No doubt the story was just a ruse Donnacona concocted to get himself, his sons and the others back home.

THE PLAN FAILED. Donnacona died in 1539 in France.

CONSPIRACY THEORISTS UNITE. Donnacona's story, however, has lived on. A few deluded optimists still hold to the dream of a bountiful land just waiting to be found. Perhaps, considering the standard of living that the country's economy now provides for Canadians, Donnacona was, unwittingly, correct!

Now for something a little different: a lie that did die
—and took the environmental movement with it for a while.

DEATH DIDN'T BECOME HIM. In 1938, the world of nature suffered a great loss. Grey Owl, the "Apache Indian" who had adopted Canada (and vice versa), died at the tragically young age of 49. His death couldn't have been a surprise, though. For years, Grey Owl had pushed himself to the point of exhaustion. Worse, he was drinking heavily.

DOING WHAT NEEDED TO BE DONE. Grey Owl was a wildly popular speaker. He spoke compellingly to large audiences about his life in the wilderness. His message was always the same: We must respect all living things. The man was utterly committed to his message of conservation. Even though he was often seriously "under the influence" when he spoke, Grey Owl always gave an effective and convincing lecture.

A TRIUMPH OF STYLE OVER SUBSTANCE. Grey Owl made even more headlines after his death than he had done before. He had been a liar. He was not, in fact, an "Apache Indian." He was an Englishman who had been raised in Sussex, England, by his father's sisters. The public was outraged; Canadians were embarrassed. Everything to do with Grey Owl immediately became suspect— including, sadly, his message of caring for the environment.

DON'T THROW THE MESSAGE OUT WITH THE MESSENGER! Grey Owl may have been a fraud, but he was also well ahead of his time. Canada and the rest of the world now accept that although the man himself was a fake, his warnings about abusing our natural resources were real.

NAME THAT TOWN

CIVIC BOOSTERS. Place names have been a bit of an issue in Canada ever since Champlain asked the Iroquois what the place was called. The Natives presumed that the explorer was asking about their little village. They told him they called it "Kanata." Champlain assumed that Kanata was the name of the land, and the misnomer stuck.

IT SEEMS FITTING. The people who study such things think that the name "Canada" is a corruption of that original misunderstanding. What could be more Canadian than confusion due to bilingualism?

CANADA BY ANY OTHER NAME... But "Canada" wasn't the only name in the running for this new country. Some real doozers made the list of losers. Aren't you glad that we don't live in Tuponia (an acronym for The United Provinces of North America) or sing "O Efsiga" (a made-up word created from the first letters of England, France, Scotland, Ireland, Germany and Aboriginal)?

KANATA REMAINS. We still do have a place called Kanata in Canada. It's not far from Ottawa. A lasting tip of the hat to that early confusion.

HOGTOWN? Ever wonder why Toronto is frequently called Hogtown? In the late 1800s there were a number of pork-packing plants located there.

WHAT A LOVELY SOUND. Antigonish. The Mi'kmaq name of that Nova Scotia city is almost a poem in itself. And thank goodness the place is called that because translated to English it means "the place where branches were torn off trees by bears gathering beechnuts." Can you imagine writing *that* address on an envelope?

ONLY IN ALBERTA, YOU SAY? PITY! Where else would you find a town named after a landlady? Claresholm, Alberta, acknowledges Clare, who once ran a boarding house in the town. At the end of a workday, many of the railway workers would go back to "Clare's home." The name came to encompass the entire community.

WHAT A LAUGH. We can only speculate about the name Lac-du-Ha! Ha!, Québec. Did the voyageurs think it was a big joke, or did the name come from one of those pesky confusions that seem to run through the place names in our country?

FOR MOM. Our old friends, those first Canadian-born explorers, the La Vérendrye boys named The Pas in northern Manitoba. They came across what is now the Saskatchewan River and named it in honour of their mother, Marie-Anne Dardonneau du Pas. Their name for the river didn't stick, but the town that grew up there has been called The Pas ever since.

EDGAR ALLAN! WELCOME TO CANADA! Poe, Alberta, must have been named by someone who liked to read really dark mysteries.

THERE GOES THE NEIGHBOURHOOD! Cheapside, Ontario, is actually a new and improved version of the area's original name—Cheap Corner. A shopkeeper in the town gave it the name. Quite the marketer, that chap.

FOR DAD. Ingersoll, Ontario, is a tribute to Laura Secord's father, Major Thomas Ingersoll.

STAY AND JAW A WHILE. What trip across Canada is complete without a stop at "the place where the white man mended the cart wheel with the jawbone of the moose"? Actually, the name comes from a Cree word, *moosegaw,* which means "warm breezes." While you're in Moose Jaw, check out the tunnels under the city—a hangover, so to speak, from the days of rum-running during Prohibition.

HUH? By the way, if you're from Moose Jaw, you'll know you are a Moosichappishanissippian. If you're not from Moose Jaw, you don't need to know.

SHORTER IS BETTER. Good old Flin Flon, Manitoba, is named after a character in a 1905 novel. Thank goodness someone had the sense to shorten the name, otherwise the folks there would be living in Flintabbatey Flonatin. And that's expecting a little much of anyone.

DRINKING IN ALBERTA. Three places in Alberta were given boozy names. In the early 1900s, Marcel Cardinal made whisky on the shores of Moonshine Lake. In 1871, a standoff occurred between whisky traders and a lawman at, say it with me now, Stand Off, Alberta. And there was a whisky trading fort at Whisky Gap in 1874.

STRANGEST PIECE OF LAND

It's maybe not too surprising that the strangest piece of Canadian soil also has the strangest history.

STRANGE GEOGRAPHY. Sable Island is the highest point on the Continental Shelf that runs under the Atlantic Ocean east of the Maritimes. It's essentially a long, narrow sandbar. The barren spot is often referred to as "the Graveyard of the Atlantic," and it came by that name honestly.

STRANGER HISTORY. The first reported shipwreck on the island occurred in 1583. There have been hundreds of wrecks since then. Approximately 10,000 souls have gone to meet their maker via Sable Island. And there is rumoured to be at least $2 million in gold lying in wrecks beneath the waves surrounding the killer outcropping of land.

IT GETS STRANGER STILL. In 1598 the French decided to ship a boatload of convicts off to the New World. The captain left the prisoners on Sable Island while he supposedly searched for an appropriate new home for the bad boys. Not long after that, though, he turned up back in France, saying that storms had blown him across the Atlantic and safely home.

AND THEN...? The French government finally went back for the prisoners—after five years! Eleven of the original 50 men were still alive. They'd made homes for themselves from the carcasses of wrecked ships scattered about the island.

NO WONDER! In the 1500s, when European explorers discovered Sable Island, their maps of the place were revealing. They consistently drew the place as being *much* bigger than it actually was. A cartography problem? Maybe it was a reflection of how terrified the sailors were of the place.

WANNA BUY AN ISLAND? By 1737 a lifesaving station had been set up on Sable Island to help ensure that the ships bringing settlers to Canada actually made it here. Then in 1738 a clergyman from Boston put the island up for sale, which was interesting because he didn't own it. Good thing no one bought it!

HORSE SENSE. In the late 1700s, 60 horses were shipped to Sable Island. The animals managed considerably better than those convicts had done, and soon the island was home to a herd of wild horses. This wasn't all bad. It meant that the lifesavers stationed on Sable could simply capture their pick of the horses and tame them on an "as needed" basis.

THE TIMES THEY ARE A-CHANGIN'. The last of the lifesavers had moved off the island by the 1960s. A solar-powered lighthouse does the job now. And with all the modern navigational equipment on ships today, wrecks are rare. There are still people on the island though—a small group of scientists who monitor weather.

ANTIQUE HORSES? Wild horses remain an important part of the Sable Island community. Their isolation has created a time capsule on the hoof, so to speak. They still look like the rugged horses of centuries ago. It's illegal, and probably not very smart anyway, to disturb the wild horses. Despite their freedom and protection, the herd hasn't overrun the island. Their numbers stay around 250.

ABOUT THE AUTHOR

Barbara Smith has always collected folklore and has successfully combined it with her other passion, writing. A bestselling author of more then 20 books, she has a deep interest in social history and loves historical research so much that she'd rather "research than eat." She has taught creative writing courses at the university and college level and is a charismatic public speaker. Barbara and her husband Bob currently live in Edmonton, Alberta.